Thomas S. Fernon

No Dynasty in North America

The West between Salt Waters

Thomas S. Fernon

No Dynasty in North America
The West between Salt Waters

ISBN/EAN: 9783337138837

Printed in Europe, USA, Canada, Australia, Japan

Cover: Foto ©ninafisch / pixelio.de

More available books at **www.hansebooks.com**

No Dynasty in North America.

The West Between Salt Waters.

Hudson Bay a Free Basin Like the Gulf of Mexico.

Hudson Strait a Free Gate Like the Strait of Florida.

Manitoba Like Louisiana a Maritime State.

North America for Citizens, Not for Subjects.

The West and Its Ways Out to the Coast and In From the Ocean.

Miscellany.

BY

THOMAS S. FERNON.

FOR SALE AT

BRENTANO'S LITERARY EMPORIUM,

39 Union Square, New York.

PRICE, **FIFTY CENTS**.

No Dynasty in North America.

THE WEST BETWEEN SALT WATERS.

HUDSON BAY A FREE BASIN LIKE THE GULF OF MEXICO.

HUDSON STRAIT A FREE GATE LIKE THE
STRAIT OF FLORIDA.

MANITOBA LIKE LOUISIANA A MARITIME STATE.

NORTH AMERICA FOR CITIZENS, NOT FOR SUBJECTS.

THE WEST AND ITS WAYS OUT TO THE COAST
AND IN FROM THE OCEAN.

MISCELLANY.

BY
THOMAS S. FERNON.

PHILADELPHIA:
PRESS OF HENRY B. ASHMEAD,
Nos. 1102 and 1104 Sansom Street.
1878.

Entered according to Act of Congress, in the year 1878, by

THOMAS S. FERNON,

In the office of the Librarian of Congress, at Washington.

NO DYNASTY IN NORTH AMERICA.

CHAPTER I.

The atlas of the world contains no political outline so "ragged edged" as the Dominion of Canada, made up of misallied provinces in single file like Indians on a trail, nowhere two abreast; and of which it may be said, could the autonomic wonder be described, that Manitoba is its chest, with one lung thawed in the grain-growing summer solstice, the other lung blockaded with ice throughout the year; its waist the wasp girth of ground between Lake Superior and James Bay; Nova Scotia its heel; and Newfoundland the big toe of its "best foot put foremost" among the fishes.

The Dominion of Canada was organized contemporaneously with the military adventure of Napoleon the Third in Mexico, during the rebellion of the Potomac Rio-Grande States, 1861–65, in expectation that secession would succeed and the American Union be dissolved. To profit from this disaster France and Great Britain made mutual preparations. But the "wayward sisters" that loved secession "not wisely but too well," when they went out at the side doors open south, are reinstalled in their old places and duties under the invincible Constitution, which, to preserve liberty in the Republic and union among the States, can take shape to meet necessities, can carry guns like a ship and be reefed and unfurled like a sail, to suit the weather of the times; and the prodigal sons of secession, willing to serve the country, break bread in Washington and divide appropriations in Congress with representatives of the States that continued steadfast; and so the four quarters of the country, named after the cardinal points, are all cemented in the joints dovetailed in the Union shield, and every State is a standard star on the national flag.

The American citizen is always and everywhere gladdened by the ensign of his nationality; and the subject in political fetters is cheered by the stars and stripes, radiant in the ports of the world penetrated by American ships, with colors at the mast-head, free in the wind and bright against the heavens, the banner an inspiration, the background the resting place for hope. What a contrast between freedom and despotism! What a transition from bondage of the mind to liberty of speech and action! Through its flag the American Union is visible, as through the firmament the universe is comprehensible; and the harmony among the States that move in the Union is identical with the harmony among the orbs that move in space. Lift up your thoughts, oh ye politicians in Congress, and look over North America, ye rulers in Washington!

Beyond the Rio Grande neighbor Mexico is an independent Republic; whereas the Dominion north of a boundary line of many crooks and few tangents, though cradled in "great expectations," an empire in embryo, for a Prince of the House of Hanover, or some one of its choosing, is uncultivable for cereal and fibrous crops in two-thirds or more of its superficial square miles.

"Only partially thawed in summer," says the geographical chart, on the polar side of a climate line through the British Possessions; and white-bear, reindeer, and walrus, says the same chart, above a climate line described as the "northern limit of barley and trees," which crosses Slave Lake and intersects Hudson Bay near the mouth of Nelson River.

The arctic highlands and islands and the icy seas and sounds between Alaska and Baffin Bay, and from the sixtieth parallel to the pole, may be considered British territory to expand the circumference of empire, and perhaps commend the Dominion to adventurous trappers, sanguine fur traders, and rash navigators in search of the magnetic point and the northwest passage; but for governmental purposes these considerations are of minimum account, even though the Esquimaux be assessed as tributers for mining for fishes in fissures in the ice.

And Europeans, when they compare localities in high latitudes in North America with localities on corresponding lines in their own country, ought always credit their milder home climate to the Gulf Stream which passes a tepid river between banks of colder water from the Florida Strait to the British islands, and via the North Sea to Norway; whilst the arctic current, with Greenland's icebergs adrift in its waters, cold almost to the freezing point, prolongs the embargo of winter in the St. Lawrence, and defers the opening of navigation to Quebec and Montreal till more than half the season of spring, always a busy time, is past and gone.

Moreover, it is wicked, because it is deception, to inscribe on a map of the Dominion of Canada "latitude of London 50° 30′" athwart Lake Winnipeg, where in midwinter the mercury sinks to fifty degrees below zero, and has been cast into balls in bullet moulds, for ocular demonstration.

True, there are prairie bottoms, upland terraces, and little and large oases in the Winnipeg basin, between the international boundary fence and the isothermal limit to agriculture. And the Dominion government, with the proceeds of loans negotiated in the "mother country," is traversing Dominion territory with the Canada Pacific Railway through twenty-seven hundred (2700) miles of wilderness, from Montreal via Ottawa, Serlick, and Yellow Head Pass, to the Pacific waters. But it is, nevertheless, a fact disparaging to the Dominion that, of the Europeans who first land in Canada, many soon push on through it into the States; so an emigrant via the Dominion is an immigrant in the Union, and hence, notwithstanding that Quebec was founded in 1608, and is older than New York city, and Serlick in Manitoba was settled fifty years before Minnesota, New York city to-day contains as many inhabitants as twenty Quebecs, whereas the white population in Minnesota is more than thirty-six times the white and half-breed population of Manitoba. New York State contains a larger population than the whole Dominion of Canada, although Jacques Cartier, a French navigator, sailed up the St. Lawrence in 1535, and it was not till 1609 that Hendrick Hudson, in the Dutch service, entered the waters of New York Bay.

In British Columbia gold was discovered in 1858, twenty years ago; but Washington Territory, on the Union side of the temporary boundary fence, and which never allured gold-hunters, contains more than twice the population of its British neighbor. Why? Because one is part of the American Republic, the other is a dependency of a foreign kingdom. In one place the man is a citizen, where patent-rights are restricted to discoveries and inventions in the sciences and arts; the other is a subject who owes allegiance to a far-away dynasty, where titles are inheritable and society is portioned into castes, as railway freight is portioned into classes. Witness:

	Square Miles.	Census.	White Population.
Washington Territory,	69,994	1870	22,195
British Columbia,	213,000	1871	10,586

The Hudson Bay Company's charter, dated May 2, 1670, expired in 1859. Lord Serlick obtained a grant of land on Red River in 1811, and in 1816 he arrived at his colony with a military escort.

In 1816 the site of Chicago was in the Northwest Territory, and the Missouri Territory west of the Mississippi River was bounded on the south by the State of Louisiana, and on the north by British America. Indiana was the frontier State, admitted into the Union December 11, 1816. When, therefore, Lord Serlick visited his settlement on Red River, in 1816, via Hudson Bay and the portages between "York Factory" and Serlick, Union domain was wilderness west of Lake Michigan; for Minnesota was not organized as a Territory till March 3, 1849, and was not admitted as a State till February 26, 1857.

Comparison.	Square Miles.	Census.	Population.
Minnesota,	83,531	1870	438,257
Manitoba,	2,891,734	1871	11,963

The population at the settlements on Red River and the Assiniboin in 1843 was 5143.

In Minnesota the whites only are counted; in Manitoba, census of 1871, the half-breeds are included with the whites.

At the time of Lord Serlick's visit to Red River in 1816, there were only eighteen States in the Union, all east of Lake Michigan and the main Mississippi River, except Louisiana; whereas now there are in the Union thirty-eight States, and eleven Territories, containing more than eleven embryo States.

There will be sixty millions of inhabitants in the Union before there will be five millions of inhabitants in the Dominion; for, in the ten years ending 1871, the Provinces of Ontario, Quebec, New Brunswick, and Nova Scotia increased only 395,265, whereas, in the ten years ending in 1870, the State of Pennsylvania increased 595,941, and the Union, notwithstanding four years of sanguinary civil war, increased 7,075,877, which is more than twice the total of Dominion population.

Here is what Minnesota, Manitoba's neighbor, has done in the way of growth and increase:

Population,	1840.	1850.	1860.	1870.
Minnesota,	0	6,077	172,023	438,257

Manitoba, in 1871, contained of whites and half-breeds 11,963. This, indeed, is a contrast in increase, in considering which it is well to remember that the French fur traders had penetrated into the Red River region from Hudson Bay, and also from Lake Superior, more than a hundred years anterior to Lord Serlick's visit in 1816. Fort Bourbon, now York Fort, was built by the French, who held it from 1697 to 1714, when possession was surrendered to the English. Manitoba, therefore, cannot urge insulation as a cause of its small population, because its two routes with portages gave it as good communications to the seaboard as were available across the Allegheny Mountain to the Ohio River, prior to the opening of the Baltimore and Ohio Railroad to Wheeling, 11th January, 1853, and the Pennsylvania Railroad to Pittsburgh, 14th February, 1854. Ohio contained over two millions of population before a railway track crossed its boundary line. "The star of empire westward took its way" at a very early day across Pennsylvania and Virginia, and the frontier State was on the west bank of the Mississippi River, opposite the mouth of the Ohio River, before the railway was in public use even in England, the land of its invention and first construction. No, no, it is as a State that Manitoba may more reasonably expect to attract immigration, for the stranger from afar would then find within it the "liberty, equality, and fraternity" which he crossed the ocean to enjoy, in personal experiences and domestic comforts.

There are no flanged family shoes worn in the Union to keep the son on the father's track, like a car with flanged wheels coupled to a car ahead, for here man is free to make a self-propelling motor of his brain power; whereas to move a train, or even a car, a steam engine is a necessity. Self-reliance in mundane matters is the American mental characteristic, and the observant alien plants his boy in American ground to grow an American citizen and enjoy freedom in manhood. The scion is not expected to trudge behind his sire, who succeeded his grandsire, but, on the contrary, to strike out for himself, when moved by inward capacity for advancement.

Where there are privileged orders to be fed and kept fat for society show-beef and birds, and honors, commissions, and offices are dispensed by royal favor, or by royal proxies, the wheel of fortune is turned by hand, clean or dirty as the case may be, like the wheel of a lottery containing a few prize numbers and many blanks; but where the goddess Fortune is neither fettered nor blindfolded, and there is free admission to the industries and the professions, and all the human pursuits which employ civilized society are open opportunities to necessity and ambition, fortune has nothing to do with the choice of service, but only with the delivery of the compensations and prizes in dollars and distinctions. And hence we see in the high places in Washington and in the States, and at the head of the industries and the professions, men moved by mental power and moral worth from the ranks of the honest poor to the foremost and uppermost positions.

All men work up or down, for no sane man is content to stand still on the same step in a flight of stairs between two floors; and to move forward is to go up and to go backward is to go down. Fame must be won else it cannot be worn; fame must be built of deeds substantial as monumental stones, or it cannot be perpetuated, for fame is the evidence of things seen with the eye of the understanding; but wealth amassed by a hoarder of dollars, like a hay-stack after a mower has pitched to its top his last forkfull of grass, is apt to diminish, for farm stock must have fodder, and heirs have voracity the same as rats; expansion and contraction are parts of one law, as the up and down ends of a seesaw are parts of one board.

There is a standard measure and rule and a true balance; and persons and things measured and weighed are sometimes short, sometimes light; but despite the imperfections and inequalities in human nature, there has been no recent reaction in the progress of the world, for Christian peoples now girth the globe, and new ideas grow among the old traditions. Public opinion is a pervading power, tending more and more to a prevailing influence in cabinet, council, and camp.

Trust in God and His purposes, and meantime rely on yourself, and in honest ways strive for honorable ends. And this is true of nations as of individuals; for a nation in its governing force is one man multiplied by many, as, indeed, is the population of the earth the posterity of one mated pair—Adam and Eve. For evidence of the past look to the books, which, however imperfect, are the only witnesses that survive for history except ruins.

Before attempting to forecast probabilities, watch current events, and weigh the men in high places, as weather doctors consult the barometer, to ascertain the pressure of the atmosphere, and the thermometer, which tells the degree of temperature.

Thus the weather-vane and mercury-tube do much for man; and the equivalent of whatsoever has been accomplished is possible of repetition; and where the people are intelligent, and incumbents of office are patriotic to country and true to duty, the ends attained tend to the common good of mankind; for developments due to mental and moral causes dispel superstition and illuminate darkness.

France is a flame in a lighthouse lantern on a coast strewn with wrecks, and Paris is an illuminated clock to the capitals of Europe, where chronometers are not corrected to the sun on the meridian, but are regulated to the phases of affairs, on different faces for separated places, like a time-piece with dials showing the hour and minute in all the principal cities around the globe.

There are other eruptions besides volcanoes which bury cities, and there are subterranean fires other than those in the bowels of the earth, which make its surface tremble and its crust crack; for public opinion aroused in anger can pour out a wrath as sure to overwhelm as lava poured from a crater is certain to harden in a winding-sheet.

Under the Republic, since February, 1871, France has achieved more than appeared possible in so few years. Hence France is an exemplar for other nations, and the United States of Europe is a consummation possible to the masses, in whom there is a latent fire like electricity, which, though invisible in the atmosphere, is irresistible in the thunderbolt. And, as a storm with lightning purifies the summer air which human beings breathe into their lungs, so revolution, with its elements in anger, is a sanitary agent where dynastic abuses offend the sense of practical economy and deteriorate the public morals and political health. A dynasty is a piece of ground watered by irrigation like a cranberry patch or a rice plantation, and produces results according as it is fed with the rainfall of other land, through the works of other hands. A republic of free states is an orchard of fruit-trees; it blossoms and bears.

A plough turns a furrow and breaks the ground for a new crop. And revolution turns the subsoil uppermost to bury the weeds turned down, and give the corn planted room to grow and ripen into golden ears. Without revolution the "Dark Ages," which cover with night more than half the Christian era, would have been prolonged through more centuries. To revolution humanity is indebted for the American Union, the climax of free government, at the date of the Declaration of Independence, and also at its centennial celebration. Revolution is public opinion expressed successfully; and no government can defy or ignore public opinion with impunity, for it is everywhere the supreme power, when it approximates unanimity in judgment and action. How careful and prompt are the ambassadors and ministers of kings and queens on the chess-board of Europe, to make a case or an excuse for a transaction or a treaty! How anxious they are to make sharp practice pass for fair play! as, for instance, when Austria was told to carve two bones off Turkey, through muscles and sinews, the Berlin Congress gave the appropriation the appearance of an European mandate rouged in the interest of peace; but Bosnia and Herzegovina were not to be assigned without protest with weapons, and the Berlin pretext deceived nobody, for nowadays important facts are communicated simultaneously to all men who read newspapers and draw conclusions. The telegram travels faster in wire to circulate the news, than the earth turns on its axis to greet the sun; steamships straight-line the oceans, and locomotive engines race-course the continents.

The Congress of Berlin, called to consider the treaty of San Stefano, determined fewer issues than it deferred; and hence the uncertainty which prevailed before it met has not been diminished since it adjourned. International questions put off to sleep are in a condition of quiet which may be broken at any time, and the recuperated party roused refreshed for another strife. What Russia needs to satisfy its necessities—national and international—is forecasted and understood; but how many months or how many years Russia may have to wait, and how and where Russia may have to venture and strike, to reach its goal is, of course, problematical.

The cause of Russia can have but one finality; its course is to a destination not in doubt, for it is the most conspicuous objective point in the Eastern Hemisphere, by reason of its ancient time and modern date antecedents and the jealousies and cross purposes which perplex the European situation.

Unquestionably the war indemnity mentioned in the San Stefano treaty, in a clause which the Berlin Congress did not supplement, is an ember in hot ashes, where a little stirring will make a smoke and start a fire. And before the Russians recross the Balkans, homeward bound, and evacuate Varna, and leave Bulgaria among the buzzards, there are sundry settlements to be made, in which the army of occupation can coöperate with St. Petersburg like a fleet with London.

Anti-Russian diplomacy exceeds equivocation when it professes to believe that the Russian people will rest on any treaty as final and conclusive which does not assure to Russia military and naval facilities to keep the straits open to Russian ships. Nothing short of such security will satisfy Russia or make peace permanent.

And as the map of the American Union will not be finished till its northern boundary, where it is a tangent fence be taken down, and sunk out of sight where it is a water-course, neither will the map of Russia be finished till more acquisitions in Europe and in Tartary are included in its consolidated empire; for the Black Sea is in verity a bottle, of which Constantinople is the cork; the cities in the basin of the Oxus—the theatre of momentous events in past times—are, in these latter days, only way stations. The mountain water-shed between the Oxus, which flows north, and the Indus, which flows south, is the main divide between India, under the rule of a foreign country on an ocean island far away, and Khanates which are dovetailed parts of the Russian Empire, with commercial interests in common with Orenburg and Astrakhan; because it is the policy of Russia to seek and strive to Russianize wheresoever it reaches and holds fast; whereas, Great Britain has, in no sense, Anglicized India, which it manipulates as if 1,558,254 square miles of territory were a plantation, and 240,000,000 inhabitants were so many chattels, utilized for the profit of absentees, less the cost of administration.

CHAPTER II.

The 1814–15 Congress of Vienna could not be repeated; nor can any one read the proceedings of that body in Thiers' "Napoleon" without indignation that Austria, which merited so little from Napoleon's overthrow, was allotted so many spoils, largely at the expense of France. But, since 1815, Germany has been organized and Italy united; Rome is restored to the ruler of Italy, and Berlin is the court of a great power. Russia, like the United States, has a mission to prosecute and frontiers to rectify; neither of the two, however, has dreams for trans-ocean empire. England's policy has made "the rich richer and the poor poorer," till now the poor of the British Isles are the poorest among the peoples of Europe; and that British exaction in India makes human food for famine in that naturally bountiful land, official records abundantly prove and demonstrate. In "The Nineteenth Century," a London monthly review, dated August, 1878, Miss Florence Nightingale, in an article which is an indictment of Great Britain for wholesale murder, says: "In Southern India, that is, in Mysore, Bombay and Madras, our loss in one year's famine has not been far short of *six million souls!*" Austria is held together, not by a fusion of particles, like a car-wheel cast in a mould on a foundry floor, but like a wheel consisting of a hub, spokes and fellies, made by a worker in wood, and held together by an iron tire, put on by a blacksmith. Turkey made conquest in Europe with the sword, and threatened to extirpate Christian civilization. And when, finally, its reverses checked its progress, its conquests were still large, for the Black Sea was a Turkish lake, entirely surrounded with Turkish territory, till 1774, when Russia made its frontier on the Black Sea, west of the Crimea, and, in 1783, added the Crimea to its acquisitions.

Through subsequent wars between Russia and Turkey, Russia acquired more and more Black Sea border from Turkey; and so Russia obtained territory on its south side in the Black Sea basin by conquest, as the American Union obtained territory on its south side in the Mississippi basin, by purchase. And Europe and America are both bettered thereby.

What Louisiana was that Manitoba is, and what Louisiana is—a State in the Union, abutting on the Gulf of Mexico—Manitoba will be—a State of the Union abutting on Hudson Bay. Then the Union will have the sea on all sides, east, west, north and south; for its shores will be washed by the Atlantic Ocean, the Pacific Ocean, the Gulf of Mexico and Hudson Bay; and its structural anatomy will be complete with the body of the continent divided into free states, united for national objects, into a Union which has withstood the trial of foreign wars and the severer test of civil strife. There is no line for the partition of the North American Union, nor for the permanent partition of the North American Continent. The West, the core of the country, will have at command and in use facilities for communication with Lake Winnipeg via Pembina, as it now has with Lake Michigan, via Peoria, by river and canal; and with Hudson Bay, by rail, as it now has with the Gulf coast and the Atlantic coast, by rail, to all the seaports from Texas to Maine.

To be sure, there will be detractors who will disparage Hudson Bay, depreciate its navigation facilities and exaggerate its obstructions from ice; but it cannot be gainsaid that it has a summer season of open and safe navigation, and that the Hudson Bay Company did utilize it throughout its long and eventful history.

In sooth, in Smollett's "History of England," on the reign of George the Second (time 1748), a hundred and thirty years ago, it is mentioned that Parliament was petitioned "that the trade of Hudson Bay might be laid open;" but the Company, having an exclusive patent, resisted the proposition, which was given the go-by, on the ground that it would entail "public expense," the aim being then, as since, to make the St. Lawrence the commercial base of operations across the continent, on British territory. But the St Lawrence route is an open navigation for only half of the year, and its outlet is high up in the north, compared with the Erie-Canal-Hudson-River route. Hence, for Dominion interests to demur to the use of Hudson Bay for a tide-water terminus for overland rail and inland water-line traffic, will be regarded by the West, when the subject attracts its serious attention, about as if Buffalo were to protest that western traffic ought not be forwarded east from the Mississippi River, via Florida Strait.

Precisely as the western part of Pennsylvania—an eastern State—is in the Mississippi basin, and Pittsburgh has its main market in the West, so the northern parts of Minnesota and Dakota—a western State and a western Territory—are in the Winnipeg basin; and Lake Winnipeg will be put in artificial water-line communication with the Mississippi River system of boat navigation, via the Red River of the North, to the Upper Missouri and the Upper Mississippi, exactly as Lake Michigan is connected with the Mississippi River system by canal from Chicago to the Illinois River.

There is no international line between New York and San Francisco, and the international line between New Orleans and Winnipeg will be obliterated; for the water-shed between Hudson Bay and the Gulf of Mexico is a roof with little inclination and a low apex, and which sends the drainage of its north side down the Nelson River spout, and from its south side down the Mississippi River channel to a common level in seas which commingle their waters in the Atlantic Ocean, via Hudson Strait and the Strait of Florida.

The French Republic, first established in 1792, was usurped by Napoleon, who was declared First Consul in 1799, and was proclaimed Emperor and crowned by the Pope in 1804. The second Republic was organized in 1848, and Louis Napoleon was elected President; he destroyed it by the *coup d'etat* December 2, 1851; was declared Emperor December 2, 1852. Coveting the Rhine Provinces, war on Germany was declared July 15, 1870; on the 2d August he telegraphed to the Empress that at the storming of the heights of Saarbruck the Prince Imperial "Louis has received his baptism of fire." Thirty days thereafter, September 1, he surrendered with MacMahon's army at Sedan, and on the 4th September the Empire succumbed to the popular indignation, and the Republic was proclaimed, in the Hotel de Ville. And the third Republic is a field oak with roots and branches, bearing seed acorns for other soils and leaves for wreaths on decoration days.

By peace, patience and perseverance the third Republic in seven years made France prosperous and potential; and the third Republic is built to stay and stand, for it is the choice of France, over and over again confirmed, as a necessity to its harmony and happiness, against the remnants and shreds of dynastic factions made up of Bourbons, Orleanists and Buonapartists, some of whom would exterminate where not permitted to reconstruct, with old material found in ruins; the third Republic, however, is approved, vindicated and justified, as the elections continuously attest; and thus the third Republic, as developed under the quickening power of Thiers and Gambetta, and a host of steadfast men wise in experience and keen in forecast, is a covenant of promise against a background of despotism, conspicuous in its colors as a rainbow against a cloud after a storm.

The eight provinces which (including Newfoundland) make up the Dominion of Canada are hitched together behind a pilot motor called a Governor-General, appointed by the occupant of the British throne, as cars are coupled in a train behind a steam engine called a locomotive, and do not constitute a congruous governmental machine, symmetrical and homogeneous in its political parts; whereas the Union may be likened to a political planetarium, in which the States move in orbits with the harmony of the heavenly bodies, and where the Constitution, effulgent as the sun, is a source of light to the nation and a beacon of hope to man, under clouded skies, in other lands.

Nor can the Dominion machine move without friction, because it is engineered in London, through submarine wire-shafting, otherwise known as the Atlantic cable, liable to abrasion on the ridges in the ocean's floor and accident from other causes.

The States of the Union, moreover, are the offspring of a co-operative compact which has a seat of reason, inductive and deductive, in universal education in public schools of grades that rise like pyramidal steps from a base in the alphabet to a summit in the sciences, and a nervous system sensitive to right and wrong, and quick to respond to whatever concerns the common country; for no matter where menaced or by whom assailed, order must be maintained in society and unity preserved in the government; because the Union is a political body permeated and pervaded with the influences and laws of attraction, cohesion and gravitation, which jointly fit it for its mission among the nations, as the earth is adjusted and charged for perpetual motion in the universe.

The Dominion, in contradistinction to the Union, is a new evolution from an old idea conceived in Europe, and, though sent hither to hatch mischief, is impotent to realize expectations either in practice or prospect, as where a reptile hatched out of a snake's egg, put into a hen's nest to scatter a brood of chickens, was scotched before it had fangs to bite.

True, the Dominion is susceptible of congelation into a solid mass by the agency of cold in winter, when it is cemented with ice and asleep under the snow. In midsummer, however, when the Winnipeg basin is in its beauty, there is a partial thaw in the walrus region, and ice-cakes, frozen in the wind from the north pole, drift out through the sounds and channels into Baffin Bay and Davis Strait, and float down the coast in the arctic current, making the air thick with fog and the provincial nose "blue" as the sky overhead, when the weather is exceptionally clear.

And if the Dominion, in a political thaw, were to break into pieces like the principal staple of its walrus region, British Columbia would drift into the Union via Puget Sound, Manitoba would tie fast to Minnesota, and Nova Scotia and New Brunswick would enter through open doors into the sisterhood of New England States, for political worship at a common national shrine.

Halifax would then in verity be the east portal open to Europe, as San Francisco is the west portal of America open to Asia. And as Halifax is on and of the seaboard, not in nor of the St. Lawrence, it ought to aspire to be the front door of the Union rather than the side door of the Dominion, for alternative use in winter time, when the St. Lawrence, its main artery, is closed with ice against Quebec and Montreal.

Halifax, notwithstanding that it was founded in 1749, a hundred and twenty-nine years ago, is to-day surpassed in population by more than thirty cities in the United States, and by three cities in the Dominion (Quebec, Montreal and Toronto), one on Lake Ontario, two on the St. Lawrence, all rival and antagonistic to Halifax, when not under embargo from ice. Contrast Halifax, as the Atlantic end of an overland railway route through the Union to the Pacific in California, with the projected overland railway route through the Dominion to the Pacific in British Columbia. Consider Halifax as a winter harbor for its three Dominion rivals, that evade it when navigation is open, with Halifax in the "mind's eye" as a naval station, commercial dock and warehouse in the Union, at the shortest ferry across the ocean that divides the new world from the old. Halifax in the Dominion is out of its legitimate sphere, like a ship caught in ice and borne away from its true destination.

But reaction is not uncommon in subject populations, where the yoke galls man, wisely made less patient than the ox, so that he may emancipate himself out of servitude to mortals of kindred clay, mould and manufacture, for sometimes the loftiest in the sight of the world are the lowliest seen from heaven. The words devil and tyrant are synonymous, because both typify the spirit of evil; and as it is meritorious to cast out a devil, so is it meritorious to overthrow a tyrant or a despotism. Therefore, where there is oppression, revolution is a righteous remedy; and forced provincial allegiance is oppression, because the provincial condition differs from the national condition as apprenticeship differs from journeymanship, with the option of mastership open with conditions common to all. In the Union a citizen may be content to vote, or he may aspire to candidateship, as an apprentice, after having served out his time, may be content to work for an employer or aspire to mastership in his calling or art; and Nova Scotia, having first refused to enter the Dominion, subsequently consented to be counted in with Quebec and Ontario, with which provinces it has little affiliation and not much intertrade. Indeed, in the company of the cities of Quebec and Montreal at Ottawa, Halifax is not unlike a third person present where there are two friends mutually anxious for a private conversation.

New Brunswick and Maine abut against each other, divided by a treaty fence, the first a province with a population of 285,594 in 1871, the latter a State with a population of 626,915 in 1870. New Brunswick was settled by the French in 1639. Maine was admitted into the Union in 1820.

Nova Scotia was visited by Europeans in 1497 and colonized in 1604, sixteen years before the first settlement in Massachusetts was made by the Puritans at Plymouth Rock. Nova Scotia, too, has developed coal deposits, Massachusetts has none; and yet in 1870 Massachusetts contained 1,457,351 of population on 7800 square miles of territory, against 387,800 of population in Nova Scotia on 18,600 square miles of territory. Boston, the principal city of Massachusetts, has New York and the Hudson River between it and the West, its main market, and back of Boston is Montreal, with communications west into the interior and east to the seacoast. Contrast Massachusetts with Nova Scotia, Boston with Halifax, and credit the difference in favor of the American citizen over the British subject, to the political circumstance that Massachusetts is a sovereign State loyal to free institutions, Nova Scotia a subject colony allegiant to a foreign kingdom twenty-five hundred miles away.

The "United Kingdom of Great Britain and Ireland" contains Britons in England, Scotland and Wales, and Irishmen in Ireland. But a Nova Scotian in the Dominion of Canada is a provincialist, and the Dominion is a colonial dependence, not an independent nation.

In 1283 Wales was finally subdued by England and annexed by conquest; and yet there are at this day thousands in Wales who use the ancestral tongue and do not understand the English language. The Scotchman is never an Englishman, though he may be more pronouncedly British than English or Welsh Britons.

In the Union the native-born and the adopted from abroad bear one common name—American citizen. The American race, made up of many breeds and crosses by immigration and intermarriage (but not by invasion like that of William the Norman, who stayed where he conquered), dominates North America with free institutions, alongside of which the European transplant will fail of propagation and die of frost in the bud.

Hudson Bay is to the hydrographic basin of Lake Winnipeg, which discharges its waters down the Nelson River, precisely what the Gulf of Mexico is to the basin bounded on the east and west by the Rocky and Allegheny Mountains, which sends its waters down the Mississippi River.

And Hudson Strait is the seagate of the Saskatchewan Valley via Lake Winnipeg, as Florida Strait is the seagate of the Mississippi Valley via the Gulf of Mexico.

The St. Lawrence is a narrow basin, and the group of connected lakes which empty into it, albeit they are inland seas in a fresh-water navigation sense, drains but an inconsiderable area of Dominion territory, compared with the area of Manitoba territory in the basin of Lake Winnipeg.

Moreover, Lake Erie, which is the distributing pool of the three lakes west and northwest of it, is connected with the Hudson River by the famous Erie Canal—an artificial work equivalent to a river in capacity and importance; and exactly as Lake Erie is connected with the Hudson River by a water-line of cheap and easy navigation, so may Lake Winnipeg be connected with the Mississippi River system of boat navigation via the Red River of the North, and, it may be, Lake Traverse and the Minnesota River Valley. From Lake Traverse, considered as a summit reservoir, the descent north to Lake Winnipeg is only 366 feet, and the descent south to the Mississippi River at the mouth of Minnesota River is only 299 feet. The moderate altitude of the Lake Traverse summit-level establishes the practicality of artificial navigation between the Minnesota River and the Red River of the North; but as the paramount consideration is a boat communication between the Mississippi River and Lake Winnipeg, the best route is a question which only intelligent engineering and summit-level water supply can decide.

Here are the elevations above sea-level:—

	Feet.
Lake Traverse, at head-waters of Minnesota River and the Red River of the North,	994
Lake Winnipeg, into which Red River empties,	628
Difference of elevation in about 650 miles distance,	366
Lake Traverse, as before,	994
Mississippi River, at mouth of Minnesota River,	695
Difference of elevation in 256 miles,	299
Red River, low-water mark, at Moorhead, where Northern Pacific Railroad crosses it,	875
Lake Winnipeg, as before,	628
Red River, at Moorhead, above Lake Winnipeg,	247
Lake Traverse, as before,	994
Red River, at Moorhead, as before,	875
Elevation of Lake Traverse above Red River, at Moorhead,	119

Moorhead is the head of steamboat navigation and Breckenridge the head of boat navigation on the Red River of the North.

Canal excavation in the prairie bottom into which the Red River of the North cut its channel would be easy work, and would shorten distance *south* of Moorhead.

Indeed, by a bold cut, like the one through the peninsula summit on the Chesapeake and Delaware Canal, a great saving of distance may be accomplished between the Red River of the North and the Mississippi and Missouri Rivers, or either of them. Canals that connect navigable waters have lost none of their consequence, but, on the contrary, annually acquire additional importance, as witness the Delaware and Raritan Canal between Philadelphia and New York, the Chesapeake and Delaware Canal, the Erie Canal, the Welland Canal, and the Illinois and Lake Michigan Canal.

The Welland Canal, a Dominion work which connects Lake Ontario with Lake Erie, has 330 feet of lockage in 27 miles of distance ; and so there are 31 more feet of elevation between Lakes Ontario and Erie than there are between the Mississippi River at the mouth of the Minnesota River and Traverse Lake, in a distance of 256 miles, and 211 more feet of elevation between Lakes Ontario and Erie than between Traverse Lake and Red River at Moorhead.

The Red River of the North has an average descent of less than seven inches in the mile; is navigable for steamboats 275 miles, and available for small boats and barges a longer distance. The Red River of the North can be utilized for the joint accommodation and mutual interest of Winnipeg, Pembina and St. Paul, and other centres of inland intertrade. Railroad bridges across it, but a few feet above high-water mark, can be elevated or provided with draws as on other rivers.

The Northwest had a very small population when the Erie Canal was opened in 1825, but look now at its tonnage and consider its importance as an artery of trade. And from Albany and Buffalo turn to St. Paul and Winnipeg; cast the horoscope of Minnesota, and discern first a million, next two millions, and after that more millions of population, with St. Paul expanded into an emporium of trade correspondingly conspicuous, boats plying the navigable water route and cars speeding the railway track between St. Paul and Winnipeg; Manitoba a State of the Union, and the population of the Mississippi Valley counted by more millions than are at this time in North America, north of Mexico; not crowded as in China proper, however, where in an area of 1,534,953 square miles there are 405,213,152 human beings, the territory occupied being less than half the size of the United States; and where, in the province of Ganhwuy, on 58,468 square miles, there were years ago 36,596,858 inhabitants; as close together and densely packed almost as honey bees in a hive, and not unlike the honey-bee-housekeepers in industry to provide and economy to save; but in the ratio of Europe west of the longitude of Belgrade and Warsaw, comprising Germany, Italy, France, Spain, Belgium, Holland, and Great Britain.

Nor is there fancy or exaggeration in this prospect; for already in matters appertaining to middle North America the word West—a term of magnitude like the term East in Europe applied to Asia—has absorbed the far west, southwest and northwest, and, along with the basin of the Mississippi River, includes the basins of the lakes west of Niagara Falls, and all the region between salt water in the Gulf of Mexico and Hudson Bay.

From Washington, New Mexico and Montana, and all between, are in the West; as from London, Hindostan and Siberia, and all between and beyond, are in the East.

The imagination is not chargeable with extravagance where prediction has been surpassed by performance and dreams have been realized in persons and things substantial.

Consider: A zone checkered with States across the continent where it is three thousand miles across, between the Atlantic and Pacific oceans; an interior basin, with thirty-six degrees of longitude between its rim in the Alleghany Mountain in Pennsylvania and the Rocky Mountains in Montana; its diameter one-tenth the circumference of the globe; its area ten times the size of Great Britain and Ireland, and six times the size of France; and which interior basin between mountain watersheds, if peopled in the ratio per square mile of France in 1872, would contain 216,000,000 of inhabitants; a basin dotted with cities from Pittsburgh to Denver, from New Orleans to St. Paul, into which cities are gathered for market the plenteous harvests from prairies and plains, from valleys with rivers in their laps, and from table lands among the mountains; a belt of earth made luxuriant and bountiful by nature, containing millions of acres under tillage, producing crops not equalled in other climes, and millions of acres open for settlement and cultivation to immigrants from foreign lands, and to native citizens prone to withdraw from large towns and small farms, to enjoy a preferred life on the frontier, remote from neighborhood and noise.

CHAPTER III.

At the beginning of the present century there was no State west of Pennsylvania, north of the Ohio River. Since January 1, 1802, twenty-two new States have been admitted into the Union—one for every three years. At the date mentioned, Pennsylvania was the frontier State on the fortieth parallel of north latitude; but there are now on that geographical line, west of the "Keystone" of the original thirteen States that won independence and framed the Constitution—twin achievements and a double fame—eight States and one Territory, admitted at these dates, to wit:

Ohio,	1802	Missouri,	1821	Nevada,	1864
Indiana,	1816	Kansas,	1861	California,	1850
Illinois,	1818	Colorado,	1876	Utah, Ter.,	1850

North of the fortieth parallel, since 1800, there have been six States and six Territories admitted, at these dates, to wit:

Michigan,	1837	Nebraska,	1867	Idaho, Ter.,	1863
Wisconsin,	1847	Oregon,	1859	Washington, Ter.,	1853
Minnesota,	1857	Dakota, Ter.,	1861	Wyoming, Ter.,	1868
Iowa,	1845	Montana, Ter.,	1864	Alaska, Ter.,	1868

Area of the thirteen original States, . . 318,572 square miles.
Area of the thirty-eight States and eleven
    Territories, ... 3,580,238 "

In 1800 there were sixteen States in the Union, and the
    population was 5,308,483
In 1870 there were thirty-seven States and twelve Territories in the Union, and the population was . . 38,558,371
In 1878 there are thirty-eight States and eleven Territories in the Union, and the estimated population is 47,000,000

Minnesota State and Dakota Territory both abut on Manitoba; and how rapidly the public lands in Minnesota and Dakota are being disposed of by the United States appears in the following comparative statement for the fiscal years ended June 30, 1877, and June 30, 1878, the same price per acre prevailing in both years:

	Total, 1878.	Total, 1877.	Increase.
Minnesota,	$1,041,203 12	$279,847 02	$761,356 10
Dakota,	1,461,801 73	218,378 20	1,243,423 53
Total,	$2,503,004 85	$498,225 22	$2,004,779 63

Increase in one year, four hundred and two (402) per cent.

In British America a very large percentage of the territory is uncultivable; and north of the sixtieth parallel of latitude the population will always be exceedingly sparse, if human beings only be enumerated, and migratory fauna, fish and fowl not counted.

South of Texas the coast lines converge to the Isthmus of Tehuantepec, and at the Isthmus of Panama they are but a span apart.

In the manifested destiny of nations North America is reserved for free institutions, for within it monarchy has perished in ignominy each time that it was tried; and the principal success in North America is the Republic of the United States, which comprises its best parts, and will include more and more of it, from time to time, howsoever British diplomacy may plot to prevent. For no dynasty can be exalted in America, where the supreme power is in the people, who put lunatics in infirmaries, and disbelieve in thrones and titles, and where kings and princes are tolerated only in mimic parts in theatrical amusements. Aged penitents who were peculators and speculators before fortune made them conservatives, sycophants destitute of manhood pride, and title-worshipping snobs and obsequious flunkeys may pretend otherwise, and ask for more license from London; but the precedents furnished by Mexico are fitted for Canada.

Personally, Maximilian was unexceptionable; but politically, he was intolerable, and in the order of events fell a victim to one of the messengers of death imported in his behalf to make Mexicans his subjects by force of arms. Subjects in America, forsooth! The word may be blotted out of the politics of Europe, for the citizen may succeed the subject in Europe, as well outside as inside of France, where all forms of government have had trial in peace and in war, and where the Republic, which, in 1870, succeeded the empire, is a pronounced success, with a record that is a marvel among the nations.

Mexico, as a Republic, has a mission in America, where the two Republics do not jostle each other, for there is room for two, side by side. The city of Mexico is well situated for communication with the interior country and the sea coasts; whereas, Ottawa, the capital of the temporary Dominion of Canada, distant only fifty-five miles from Ogdensburg, in the State of New York, will be twenty-six hundred miles distant from the Pacific waters, by the Canada Pacific Railway, when built, from Ottawa to Port Moody, in British Columbia! The railways of the Dominion, financially considered, may have had blossoms in prospectuses, but have not had fruits in profits; but, bad as the fiscal showing is in the official reports of roads years in use, there will be still less comfort derived from the earnings of the Canada Pacific Railway, to offset its prodigious cost; for its route, like much of the route of the Inter-Colonial Railway, is through a region of minimum local resources; and what its through traffic is to consist of, and whence it is to come, is an inquiry adjourned till after it shall have been inaugurated, and then—what? Why, then, the farce annually repeated at the Canada Grand Trunk Railway meeting will be played simultaneously on two stages, where pay-roll officials are the actors and investors make up the audience of dupes.

A railway from Frazer River southward to a connection with a line to San Francisco would be worth more to British Columbia than the Canada Pacific Railway can be, *east* of Manitoba; and the same is true of Manitoba and the railway via Winnipeg and Pembina, against the Canada Pacific Railway extended east of the Red River of the North to Ottawa.

Contemplate the intertrade of the Atlantic States, and think of British Columbia along with Washington Territory and the States of

Oregon and California. Think of the intertrade between Ohio river towns and New Orleans and throughout the Mississippi basin, from Pittsburgh to Denver, and consider Manitoba as a State in sympathy with Minnesota and in coöperation with other States, down to the Gulf of Mexico. From Manitoba the outlook is south, not east, and the interest of Manitoba is—and its aspirations ought to be—to advance from an inland province into a maritime State like Louisiana.

Indeed, it is a hypothesis founded on ancient watermarks and topographical indications that time was when the surface of Lake Winnipeg was higher than its present level, the prairie bottom of Manitoba under water, and the outflow to the sea via Traverse Lake and down the Minnesota valley into the Mississippi River, till a break was made through the ridge which walled in the great reservoir on its north side, and the channel in which flows Nelson River was opened to Hudson Bay, now Middle Sea.

Chautauqua Lake, in the southwest corner of New York, is 1306 feet above the level of the sea and 738 feet above the level of Lake Erie, from which it is only seven miles distant; but Chautauqua Lake discharges its waters not into Lake Erie, seven miles distant, but into the Gulf of Mexico, twenty-four hundred miles away, via the Alleghany, Ohio and Mississippi Rivers.

But, whether the waters of Lake Winnipeg priorily flowed south, down a gentle incline, or escaped north, down falls and rapids, the substantial fact remains, that Manitoba may be put in navigable communication with the Mississippi River, so that boats may be passed from Winnipeg to St. Paul, and even from Hudson Bay to the Gulf of Mexico; as boats can now navigate a continuous water-route between New Orleans and Quebec, via the Illinois River and the canal thence to Chicago, whence the way is open to the lower St. Lawrence.

Lake Winnipeg may be made a commercial dock or pool like Lake Erie, if its navigation be connected by canal with the river navigation of the Mississippi and Missouri Rivers, as Lake Erie is connected with tide-water in the St. Lawrence, via the Welland Canal, and with the Hudson River by the Erie Canal, a work to which New York State is indebted for its "empire" rank, and New York city for its commercial supremacy.

The Saskatchewan and the Missouri are kindred rivers, whose sources are near together in the Rocky Mountains, and the communities along the sister river banks will develop affinities for intertrade that will promote commercial intercourse and political co-partnership; for the Frazer River and the Columbia River, the Missouri River and the Saskatchewan River, like the rivers which flow from fountains among the peaks of the Allegheny Mountain, down both its sides, all drain parts of one country, pervaded by a common sympathy, which an artificial line cannot dissever nor distract.

St. Paul is an important steamboat terminus and a conspicuous centre of railway traffic. From St. Paul there are 1940 miles of steamboat navigation southward to New Orleans, and 1913 miles of steamboat navigation eastward to Pittsburgh. On the Mississippi river and its principal tributaries there are 16,674 miles of river navigation. Verily, the Mississippi River system is an inland wonder.

Surely to Manitoba it is of paramount importance that from Lake Winnipeg there should be a boat navigation to the Mississippi River, as there is from Lake Michigan a boat navigation to the Mississippi River. The level of Traverse Lake is only 299 feet above the Mississippi River at St. Paul, and 366 feet above Lake Winnipeg; but only 119 feet, or thirty-three per cent. of the latter difference would have to be overcome by lockage, because to Moorhead the Red River of the North is a steamboat navigation, and at Moorhead the surface of Red River is 247 feet above its surface at its mouth in Lake Winnipeg.

Between Buffalo and Albany, on the famous Erie Canal, there are 642 feet of lockage, and from Lake Erie to Montreal there are 568 feet of lockage.

Between the head of steamboat navigation at Moorhead, on the Red River of the North, and the head of navigation on the Mississippi River at the mouth of the Minnesota River, the lockage would be only 418 feet, 150 feet less than the lockage between the Lake Erie head of the Welland Canal and Montreal on the St. Lawrence.

No one can examine the question of the basin of the Mississippi main river and its tributaries and not be convinced that the Red River of the North, which is divided from the affluents of the Mississippi River and the Missouri River by a phenomenally low prairie divide with innumerable lakes, will be connected by canal with the navigable streams so very near it on both sides, east and west.

Between Fort Garry, on Red River, and Lake Superior, the Dominion government has in operation a route consisting of 140 miles of road, 8 miles of portages and 304 miles of water navigation; total length 452 miles. The summit-level swamp on this route, distant 74 miles from Prince Arthur Landing, Lake Superior, is 1483 feet above the level of the sea, and 489 feet higher than Lake Traverse above the sea; so that from the swamp summit to Lake Superior, which latter is 600 feet above the sea, there is a descent of 883 feet, against 299 feet from Lake Traverse summit to the Mississippi River.

During the year ended June 30, 1876, there were carried over the Dominion summer route, between Lake Superior and Fort Garry,

2172 passengers, a small number, considering the force employed on the Canada Pacific Railway, additional to resident population, emigrants going out and immigrants coming in.

During the year ended June 30, 1876, the Northern Pacific Railroad carried 3645 passengers to and 6951 passengers from Moorhead on Red River.

By the Canada Pacific Railway route the distance from Fort Garry on Red River to Lake Superior at Fort William is 410 miles. From Fort Garry the air-line distance is 50 miles less to Duluth in Minnesota than to Fort William in Ontario.

From Fort Garry the railroad distances south and east are: To the Minnesota line, by the Pembina branch, 85 miles; to Breckenridge on Red River, 287 miles; to St. Paul on the Mississippi River, 504 miles; from St. Paul to Chicago, 409 miles; Fort Garry via Breckenridge and St. Paul to Chicago, 913 miles. The distance by rail between Chicago and Fort Garry can be shortened a hundred miles via Milwaukee and Thomson.

From Chicago to New York by shortest route via Pittsburgh and Philadelphia, operated by the Pennsylvania Railroad Company, the distance is 913 miles, precisely the same as the distance from Chicago via St. Paul and Breckenridge to lower Fort Garry, where the Canada Pacific Railway crosses Red River. Total distance from Fort Garry through Breckenridge, St. Paul, Chicago and Philadelphia, to New York city, 1826 miles. From Fort Garry to Halifax by Canada Pacific and Intercolonial Railways via Ottawa, Montreal and Quebec, the distance is 2308 miles, all on Dominion territory.

As, however, the St. Lawrence is ice-bound for half the year, comprising a part of autumn, the whole of winter, and more than two-thirds of spring, the ports of Montreal and Quebec are of course closed to navigation all that time; and as Halifax is 482 miles farther distant than New York city from Fort Garry, the foreign trade of Manitoba, if allowed to choose its own channel, will be across Minnesota and through Union seaports to Europe.

The ambition to have a through route on Dominion territory is, therefore, beset with drawbacks to realization insurmountable in practice. The untrammelled intertrade between the States of the Union will not be overlooked by Manitoba, which will hardly consent to be "bottled" for political reasons formulated at Ottawa, by a propaganda that would transplant to the new world the political society shams of the old world, outside of Switzerland and France.

Why should England endure a titled aristocracy that withholds from cultivation millions of acres in a country that imports much of its breadstuffs, pays but little tax on landed estate, arrogates social superiority, enjoys the highest office-honors, and revels in fashionable dissipation, with wealth to command the luxuries of life, where comforts are so scarce among the masses?

In the Union only commodities are classified, and all honors and opportunities are open to free competition. In Great Britain title and position are inherited and transmitted, and there the ballot can do but little good until the laws of primogeniture and entail be repealed.

Under a dynasty, man-power, horse-power, and steam-power are all alike considered available for utilization in the economy of government. And thus man, "immortal man, made in the image of his Maker," is degraded to a brute and equated to a machine. His natural rights are restricted beyond the necessities of a legal code essential for order and administration, and his privileges are circumscribed to a minimum radius of option; for he is the subject of the crown, and is told to be thankful for the royal condescension that makes life bearable, under conditions which provide palaces and parks for inheritors of ancestral distinctions, life tenures, and entailed estates, and reduce the millions to an existence beset with more penalties than compensations, often clouded by day, seldom bright by night; a purgatorial life between a worse condition under barbarism and a better condition under uniform rights.

In a republic birthright is equality under the law, and free competition for the public offices and honors and in the professions and pursuits.

In a monarchy titles and honors are reserved out of the common stock of the state, which in a republic comprises the whole people, whereas in a monarchy the state is an establishment administered and enjoyed by a law-favored class; an aristocracy not of mind or superiority of brain capacity, but of birth under a dynastic code wherein prerogatives are perpetuated, contrary to the republican practice and the wise course of nature which with impartial hand scatters its gifts in the soils and rocks, where they reward the finder according as he earns success by his own industry and effort.

The seasons come and go, and after every departure there is a return in the circle run, for nature has fixed laws which survive vicissitudes in the weather; the day runs its rounds to true time, and only the air is fickle in its temperature.

Human government is comparative, and at best imperfect, because ambitious man is prone to discontent, and from a step mounted strives to climb a step higher and is overturned; for a ladder must have two rests, one on the ground, the other against an object to prop its elevated end; and if a pit under it be opened or its support be removed, its own gravity will cause it to fall; so government must be founded in impartial justice, and be supported by public opinion, else it will incline from the upright, and in its tumble down take with it to the ground those who made of it a ladder for selfish exaltation, in forgetfulness of the special providence that its top round was below the lookout summit where public opinion, in a republic, is a law of gravitation to bad men who aspire to leadership among the people. In a dynasty there is a standing army of bayonets; in a republic the adult population is armed with the ballot, which at the poll is the equivalent of a ball in battle.

Louisiana is a conspicuous State in the Union by reason of its sugar and cotton plantations, and because it abuts on the Gulf of Mexico and contains the focus of Mississippi River and seaboard and trans-Atlantic trade in the city of New Orleans, which occupies one of the most commanding sites on the world's waters, for domestic and foreign trade, having thousands of miles of steamboat navigation on the fresh-water rivers in its rear, and tens of thousands of miles of steamship navigation in the ocean currents on its front and flanks.

As a State in the Union, Manitoba would attract observation and acquire distinction, because it abuts on Hudson Bay or Middle Sea, which is a summer-door to the ocean from Minnesota and the West, but which, notwithstanding British professions of free trade when an Englishman opens his mouth in Washington, is shut and barred to force trade down the St. Lawrence. Consider the geographical situation of Hudson Bay, which continues the sea into the West more than half way across the Canada main, between the Atlantic and Pacific Oceans. With Hudson Bay declared a free and open sea, Manitoba as a maritime State would profit from a back-door on the north open to Europe, as Louisiana profits from a front-door on the south open to the West Indies and all the Atlantic coasts.

Manitoba, as one of six States across the Union, where its axle would then turn on six wheels, Louisiana, Arkansas, Missouri, Iowa, Minnesota, and Manitoba, between two seas, one called a bay, the other a gulf, would have communication in all directions between the haunts of Newfoundland whales and Aleutian seals, tropical alligators and polar bears.

True, Nelson River has rapids and falls, and so has the St. Lawrence and other lake and river routes, rapids and falls; but these natural obstructions to navigation have been overcome by the judicious expenditure of money in works engineered with skill; and thus through ways of art, works of nature are utilized. And compared with what has been expended, and wisely expended, on artificial aids to navigation between Lake Superior and tidewater in the St. Lawrence, the sum needed would be small, to provide artificial aids to navigation from Lake Winnipeg to Hudson Bay.

It is but a short distance from Lake Winnipeg to Hudson Bay, from Lake Superior to James Bay. And if the Canada Pacific Railway be located on the north side of Lake Nipigon, a short branch road would suffice to reach a harbor on James Bay.

Apart from British considerations, which in the Dominion run counter to the logic of American events, it is its commercial merit as a portage railway between the Gulf of Georgia and Hudson Bay, through British Columbia and Manitoba, that gives the Canada Pacific Railway much of the interest it awakens. And as it is certain that Montreal will advocate branches from the Canada Pacific main line to ports on near-by tidewaters, Montreal cannot demur if Manitoba insist on a branch road to a terminus on the James Bay arm of the ocean, so very much nearer than tidewater in the St. Lawrence.

The railway from Fort Garry to a junction with a Minnesota road from St. Paul to St. Vincent, opposite Pembina, will, at the boundary line, put Manitoba in railway communication with Minnesota, Winnipeg with St. Paul, and the railway network of the Mississippi States—a consideration which a Manitoban will not overlook, but which he will be careful to weigh and turn to account.

A link of road from the junction of the Northern Pacific with the Duluth and St. Paul line at Thomson, to the Canada Pacific Railway on high ground west of Fort William, where it deflects northward and possibly will pass around Lake Nipigon, would make a seaport on James Bay, to be called *Middlesea*, the northern terminus of the Mississippi railway system, which now has its northernmost station at Duluth, Lake Superior, a fresh-water reservoir, not a part of the salt-water sea like James Bay.

Undoubtedly Middlesea will be a grain port—a sort of Odessa—measured by its bushels, on James Bay, whence Hudson Strait opens a way to Europe, on the old track of the Hudson Bay Company's ships, where the season of navigation has not been shortened.

The incorporation of British Columbia and Manitoba with Ontario, Quebec, New Brunswick, Nova Scotia, and Prince Edward's Island, was a political misalliance that will make incompatibility manifest in domestic discord; for whilst Manitoba will have warm fellowship with Minnesota, it will have only cold acquaintance with lower Ontario and Quebec; and whilst British Columbia will cultivate intimate relations with the Pacific States, and especially with the city of San Francisco, the Atlantic provinces of the Dominion will remain strangers to it, for Halifax is farther from it than is New York city. And the Canada Pacific Railway, failing to cause an exodus into the wilderness of rigors, but serving as well to carry dissatisfied emigrants thence as deceived immigrants thither, will disappoint the sanguine temperaments of London, where

> " 'Tis distance lends enchantment to the view,"
> And gilds the iceberg with the guinea's hue.

Between Lake Superior and James Bay a temporary boundary, beyond which the Dominion may not go, is indicated in probabilities which are as blossoms of future fruits, depending for maturity on season, circumstance and time.

A subject is not a citizen; a subject is required to be allegiant to a dynasty to which are mortgaged the natural rights of his posterity, from generation to generation; a citizen, on the contrary, is loyal to his government, of which he is a vital part, and which he operates through proxies appointed by the ballot that thinks and counts, and therein differs from the bayonet, which is only a tool; and as the judicious citizen is careful of his own body, to preserve his health and prolong his life, so is he also watchful of the republic, especially when danger lowers and a crisis impends, ready and anxious with the remedy which the ballot contains, to cure abuses that degrade localities and deteriorate the civil service.

Since the first pair were cast out of Eden, and Adam was told "to till the ground from whence he was taken," there has been no paradise on the earth. But a republic approximates paradise, compared with other governments, as Christian piety approximates perfection, compared with Turkish brutality and Mahometan absolutism.

Personal government is despotism, illustrated in the First and the Third—the big and the little Napoleon—who both waged war for aggression, and both caused the temporary prostration of France at enormous cost in treasure and life. And for what? *Vain glory!*

And so-called responsible government, where there is a crown or life tenure, with a right of succession, and an aristocracy with personal prerogatives and class privileges, is a "counterfeit presentment" of constitutional power, because it represents only a portion of the people ruled, and where all are not represented the rights of the unrepresented are usurped.

In Europe, France and Switzerland excepted, the masses, deprived of the exercise of rights essential to free and equal government, are graduated in the scale of life farther below their oppressors, who rule over them, than they are marked above the flocks and herds, notwithstanding that, in the order of nature, the prince and the peasant die by the same process—dissolve into common dust—and go to judgment together on their merits.

The American citizen, from the political level on which the people stand, may mount the winding stair of promotion to its topmost step, and there elevated wield the presidency of the United States; but at the end of his term he descends from his high office of human greatness, and, having witnessed the inauguration of his legal successor, quietly resumes his citizenship, without a pension or other reward than the affections of a constituency faithfully served, and which he reciprocates and is grateful for.

In a province where the subject owes allegiance to a foreign power, there is a condition of dependence not congenial to manhood aspirations for distinction and progress. And it is called "recruiting the aristocracy from the ranks," when a commoner, no matter for what reason, is given a title to distinguish him from his fellows. But prefixion and suffixion are dropped from the immortal names best known throughout the world, as, for instance, "George Washington," who was commander-in-chief of the armies during the revolution, and the first President of the United States. The world identifies indelible names with indelible deeds, and does not cite titles when it quotes heroes and benefactors. Why, then, are titles made inheritances in kingdoms? Because they represent civil prerogatives and social distinctions, reserved from the people despoiled of their rights! The unrest of the people makes the dynasties of the Old World shake like a cradle on rockers. And for a cause of the prevailing unrest look at the inequalities in the condition of the masses, oppressed with national debts, standing armies, heavy taxes and poor pay for hard work. Intellectual superiority, where not bound or bottled, will assert itself, compel recognition, and command acceptation and admiration, too, if its tendencies be sympathetic and patriotic. Cavour, Thiers and Bismarck are three illustrious examples of individual influence in national councils in recent times.

Reigning houses in Europe do not abound in ideas, and their cost as establishments is not alone in disproportion to their availability to the state, but is equally in disproportion to the capacity of the people to pay. Retrenchment which begins by reducing the compensation of the lowliest, whose per diem is least, is false economy; for as prices go down, the purchasing power of the dollar goes up. Hence, those who escape reduction of salary by the year are benefited by the misfortunes of those who suffer reduction of compensation per day and hour.

Contrast the revenues of the royal family of Great Britain from the national treasury and other sources, with the pay-roll of all the operatives in the "black country" of Lancashire, and the cost of royalty, with its immunities and impunities, would be apparent.

In the United States abuses crop out in the newspapers, and the delinquent is discussed and retired on the black list.

In Great Britain the consequences of abuses are visited on the struggling workingman, who is the bottom rock in a social system which has more degrees and gradations than there are formations in the stratification exposed in a shaft, from the surface of the ground to the bottom of a deep mine.

In the United States the avenues of preferment are as numerous and as open as the public roads, to the honors of station and the prizes of fortune. And herein America is utterly unlike Great Britain, where there are laws of primogeniture and entail, and a nobility titled by patent right, like devices in the mechanic arts. Hence, subjects in the over-peopled countries of Europe (particularly parents of children), who look abroad over the earth in search of fields wherein opportunities invite enterprise and industry, are fortunate if they elect to train for citizenship of the United States, where the Celtic and Teutonic branches of the Caucasian race are conglomerated in a new type of advanced humanity, builders of States in a cemented Union which has a base broad as the continent and a roof higher than the clouds.

Into this Union, Alaska and the Aleutian Islands, acquired from Russia in 1867—an acquisition geographically strategic and politically significant—was the admission of latest date.

The admission of Manitoba and British Columbia will follow, because in the Dominion they insulate Alaska from its sisters, and are in political association—not with neighbors next door, with whom alliance would be the result of natural laws—but with distant relations, through unhappy contract into which they were inveigled when too weak to resist persuasion.

The retrocession of the territory ceded to Great Britain by the treaty of June 15, 1846, prior to which it had been avowed by the Polk administration that the title of the United States to the Russian line at 54° 40′ was "clear and unquestionable," will quicken a Pacific coast province into a Pacific coast State, and give the Strait of Juan de Fuca rank and consequence with the Golden Gate of San Francisco.

And Manitoba, separated from the province of Ontario by a temporary boundary line from the north side of Minnesota to the south end of James Bay, will no longer be in solitude, cold as its ice and cheerless as its north wind, for annexation will do for Manitoba what annexation did for Texas, as witness:

Population of Texas, census of 1870, . 818,579
States of Mexico on the Rio Grande river:
Population of Tamaulipas, . . . 108,514
Population of Coahuila, . . . 67,691
Population of Chihuahua, . . . 179,971
Total as per report of commission from Mexico to Philadelphia Centennial Exhibition, ... ———— 356,176

Texas in excess of three Mexican border states, 462,403

As a state of Mexico, Texas would have remained undeveloped, exactly as Manitoba has remained undeveloped under British jurisdiction, notwithstanding the attempts made to colonize it; for Texas was discovered by La Salle in 1580, and Manitoba, too, is venerable, the Hudson Bay Company's charter bearing date 1670—eleven years before Penn founded Pennsylvania—and the Serlick settlement on the Red River of the North was visited by Lord Serlick with a military escort in 1816, at which time Indiana was a border State and Illinois a Territory.

Mineral discovery, agricultural development, material progress, and widespread prosperity, have added State after State to the American Union in rapid succession, meanwhile that British territory north of the forty-ninth parallel, and Mexican territory south of the Rio Grande river, is still most of it wilderness, though explored before the thirteen British colonies became the thirteen original American States of the Union since made continental, and which now contains thirty-eight States and eleven Territories.

Truly this grand result is a glowing credit to free institutions, which tolerate no patent political classes, but treat all citizens politically alike; nowhere else are opportunities so abundant, nor is success so frequently attained by individuals endowed with mental gifts and moral worth, and who study for success with honest zeal and manly purpose, never wavering in fidelity to the Testament, the Constitution, or the common weal. The political creed of the American citizen is: Allegiance to God, the sole sovereign in nature, and of whom an earthly sovereign is a poor counterfeit, a mite in matter; faith in Christ, but not in crowns; duty to self with minimum selfishness; fidelity to the Republic, which is a panoply over North America studded with States that glow in the political firmament like stars in the azure arch beneath the spirit world of heaven overhead.

CHAPTER IV.

The basin of Lake Winnipeg is drained by rivers which flow down from the west, south and east, including the Red River of the North, that spreads its sources and affluents over large portions of Minnesota and Dakota, there interlocking on low water-sheds with tributaries of the Missouri and the Mississippi; and also including the Saskatchewan, whose headwaters are among the fountains of the Columbia River in the Rocky Mountains.

The area of Lake Winnipeg basin is 360,000 square miles, eight times the size of the State of New York, and seventy per cent. larger than the basin of the Ohio River from its source in Pennsylvania to where it disembogues in the Mississippi River at Cairo in Illinois, a distance of 1265 miles.

Lake Winnipeg basin, moreover, contains the cultivable British territory, available for agriculture, between the watershed near Lake Superior and the Rocky Mountains. To be sure, the fur-trader may penetrate farther north into the walrus region—which ought to be called the province of *Walrusia*, or reindeer reservation—but the farmer will not accompany him with his plough, for frozen ground is not arable where the sun in summer only thaws the surface of the earth and Flora pays short visits to her wild flowers.

In the early days of American discovery, France colonized a strip of territory from the mouth of the St. Lawrence via the lakes and the Ohio to the mouth of the Mississippi. And France first established forts on the inland sea afterwards called Hudson Bay; but the fortune of war deprived France of Canada, and subsequently France sold Louisiana to the United States, thereby preventing its possible conquest and occupation by a rival European power, and assuring to its inhabitants a destiny identical with the Mississippi valley States. In this transaction, which occurred in 1803, Napoleon, then Consul for life, exhibited both foresight and wisdom; for, had France been dispossessed of Louisiana by the conqueror of Canada, the trespass would have irritated the American people and provoked a war, because self-preservation, to say nothing of "manifest destiny," made it clear that the whole of the Mississippi basin should be in and of the Union. The battle of New Orleans, fought by General Andrew Jackson, January 8, 1815, is a record of what the West will do to keep the Mississippi basin intact and tight, to hold together the States within it for mutual protection and a common aim, these love-bound States meantime serving as political models for imitation by colonies subjected to foreign jurisdiction and slower growth.

The American citizen is a new graft on the Caucasian tree; the British subject is a transplant that will not bear British fruit in American soil, for nativity in the Republic is nationality, whereas the colonial condition is political bondage; nor can an intelligent, free-will native of France, Ireland, Germany, Holland, Italy, Belgium, Russia, Austria, Sweden, Denmark or Spain stay in a Canadian province and owe allegiance to England afar off, when he can move into a near-by State and become a citizen of the American Republic, where political equality dwells, and immigrants can thrive and be happy in their own homesteads.

In Manitoba no man can shut his optic nor his mental eye to the fact that the outlook south down the Mississippi is brighter and warmer and more genial than east down the St. Lawrence, to where icebergs float in fleets, fog-banks envelop the coasts, and the inhabitants, in compliment to the climate, are called "blue-noses."

Manitoba, therefore, will evolve out of a province into a State, as Texas did, and so illustrate the doctrine of evolution applied to political institutions, and as demonstrated in Louisiana in 1803, Florida in 1819, Texas in 1846, California in 1848, and Alaska in 1867, all acquisitions surpassing assessment or valuation, all evolutions since the revolution of the thirteen colonies into thirteen States, the fatherland of the twenty-five additional States admitted into the Union, east of the Hudson River and west of the Allegheny Mountain.

As a maritime State on the Hudson Bay (Middle Sea), Manitoba will not be unlike the maritime State of Louisiana on the Gulf of Mexico; for as New Orleans has communication with Europe via Florida Strait, so will the principal city of Manitoba, through a seaport in Manitoba on Hudson Bay, or in Ontario on James Bay, have communication with Europe via Hudson Strait, when open to navigation the same as the St. Lawrence, after the annual thaw which ends the embargo of inevitable ice.

In the organization of the Dominion of Canada, the province of Ontario in 1867 had assigned to it that portion of Canada included prior thereto in the province of Upper Canada. And Upper Canada ended on the west where the Hudson Bay Company's territory commenced on the east, to wit. at the Kaministiqua River, at the mouth of which is Fort William, Thunder Bay, Lake Superior. The Hudson Bay Company, whose charter, granted in 1670, expired in 1859, was bought out and succeeded by the Dominion of Canada. But Ontario claimed that its territory extended to the Rocky Mountains, if not to the Pacific Ocean, and a boundary commission was appointed to arbitrate between the Dominion of Canada and the Province of Ontario. The award of the arbitrators is dated August 3, 1878.

The new boundary established by the commission leaves James Bay at the mouth of the Albany River, thence up the said river and via Lake St. Joseph, thence to the headwaters of the English River, and thence westerly to a meridional line drawn from the most northwesterly angle of the Lake of the Woods, and thence south to the national boundary. This decision cuts into Manitoba and extends Ontario about two hundred miles west of its original limitation. What use Ontario will make of its acquisition time will unfold. Manitoba, however, will very soon enjoy unbroken rail communication between Winnipeg and St. Paul via St. Vincent, opposite Pembina. And the exclusion of Manitoba from its frontage on Lake Superior at Thunder Bay, and thence to Pigeon River at the Minnesota line, will tend to identify Manitoba more and more with Minnesota and the Mississippi valley. Not an inch of Manitoba territory is left in the basin of Lake Superior; but, on the contrary, Ontario's new boundary line runs along the west side of the watershed between Lake Superior and Winnipeg, completely insulating Manitoba from Lake Superior.

The State of Pennsylvania was not content to continue insulated from Lake Erie, and purchased territory on Lake Erie whereby it acquired a lake harbor at Erie City. Manitoba had territory and harbors on Lake Superior, but Manitoba has been this present year deprived of its Lake Superior frontier, to aggrandize Ontario! True, Manitoba still has Duluth in Minnesota for an objective point on Lake Superior, instead of a landing place on Thunder Bay in Ontario. Nevertheless, it was unkind to drive Manitoba out of the St. Lawrence basin, which includes Lake Superior and its affluents, to extend Ontario into the Winnipeg basin, even to the "most northwesterly angle of the Lake of the Woods," covering a large area of land, and lakes, and rivers, which constitute portions of the Winnipeg system of water navigation. In this diplomatic adjustment of boundary line Manitoba is the sufferer; and if Manitoba was previously distrusted at Ottawa, and therefore in precaution against possible future movements in the West, which returns its rainfall to the sea through the Mississippi and Nelson Rivers, the Province of Ontario was extended over portages, rivers and lakes to the Winnipeg River, the loyalty of Manitoba to Ottawa and royalty will hardly be increased by its severance and expulsion from the St. Lawrence basin, between Pigeon River and Thunder Bay; for now Manitoba, cut off from Lake Superior by the new frontier of Ontario, is in complete identification with Minnesota, which has a Mississippi River harbor at St. Paul, a Lake Superior harbor at Duluth, and railways in all directions.

Michigan and Wisconsin as well as Minnesota may look to James Bay for an additional outlet to the ocean; and if Ontario demur to right of way from the north shore of Lake Superior to James Bay, Ontario cannot expect to enjoy unlimited facilities in Michigan, to reach Chicago. Are not Dominion interests promoted by the ferry across Lake Michigan, between Milwaukee and Grand Haven, by the ferry across Detroit River, between Detroit and Windsor, and by the ferry across the Strait of St. Clair, between Port Huron and Sarnia? And when necessity or convenience shall require ferry accommodations between the south shore of Lake Superior, occupied jointly by Michigan and Wisconsin, and the north shore, all in Ontario, to facilitate communication with James Bay, and with Europe via Hudson Strait, will Ontario or the Dominion grant the necessary legislation for a lake ferry and a portage railway, or venture to withhold it?

Great Britain is not satisfied with the open sea route to India via the Cape of Good Hope, but fusses and blusters about the Suez Canal, as if anybody intended to shut it; and about the Euphrates valley, as if anybody not British intended to build a railroad in it, when there is better ground for a shorter route to India, from Paris, Berlin, and St. Petersburg, north of the Black Sea!

The West, which comprises the basin of the Mississippi River and the basins of the lakes west of Niagara Falls, will also comprise the basin of Nelson River; and then the West will cover and include all the territory between the salt waters in the Gulf of Mexico and Hudson Bay, and from the Allegheny Mountain, where the Atlantic slope ends, to the Rocky Mountains, where the Pacific slope begins. There is only one West in North America, and that has mountain watersheds on the east and west parallel with the two oceans, and reservoirs of seawater on the north and south.

Hudson Bay will be made available for a distributing basin in summer time. Compared with Hudson Strait the St. Lawrence route through Quebec and Ontario is a sinuous way to the sea, from the wheat belt in the West, to which England is indebted for much of its bread, as it is likewise indebted to the Union for meat to eat and cotton to wear. Great Britain, with its entailed estates and areas of cultivable land reserved from cultivation, and its titled aristocracy to support in luxury, is a heavy buyer of breadstuffs.

Among the nations where government is wise and domestic policy is far-sighted, it is the aim of each to manipulate its own ores and fibrous productions into manufactures for consumption and exportation, a discriminating practice which will tend to modify foreign commerce into intertrade in surplus commodities; for a nation will not continue to pay out for labor, in another land, money which may be distributed for labor at home. The machine-man is on his travels, busy at every World's Fair, and the distribution of labor on a new basis, not British, is his grand mission.

The original thirteen States which cut the colonial knot to terminate allegiance to Great Britain, and which, after winning with the sword the title of "free and independent States," established the Union under a Constitution framed with rare wisdom and prophetic adaptation to human wants, were all in a row along the Atlantic coast, east of Florida, afterwards acquired from Spain. Now, the Union has an ocean boundary west as well as east, and a gulf border on its south side; but the Union also needs Hudson Bay, *i. e.*, Middle Sea, for an Atlantic dock, to facilitate and cheapen intercourse and intertrade between Europe and the Mississippi, the Rocky Mountains and the Pacific States, Manitoba and British Columbia, as States of the Union, likewise inclusive. Then, the Union will have two seas for boundary docks, and axis ends midway between its two ocean shores; and from its two principal inland cities, Chicago and St. Louis, marts of rapid and vigorous growth, straight lines drawn to the four cardinal points will all intersect tidewaters, open to free navigation around the world.

When head winds delayed the mariner, and blew his ship off its course, long voyages, as living persons can testify, were tedious undertakings; but, nowadays, the steamship runs to schedule time, on paths across the waters, as the locomotive engine runs to schedule on railways overland, whereby the time-table and the time-piece regulate the affairs of foreign trade conducted under treaties; and so, in a practical dollar sense, apart from the more elevating intellectualities and sublimer divinities of the theme, the intertrade movement is but an international show held in a single spot, as in Fairmount Park, Philadelphia, in 1876, magnified and expanded to the true areas of the nations and the true quantities and values of the import and export trade over the whole earth.

And the nations that were separated by distances in miles, beset with difficulties which delayed transportation and increased its cost, can, in these times, advanced into the interior of civilization, deliver the commodities of intertrade by sure, swift and cheap conveyance, on contracts and messages passed through submarine cables and overland wires that "put a girdle round about the earth" in considerably less than Puck's minimum of "forty minutes."

Although the fortune of war deprived Great Britain of thirteen colonies, which became thirteen States, containing 318,572 square miles of surface, since expanded into thirty-eight States and eleven Territories, Great Britain plans and builds railways to keep the provinces of the Dominion together with iron bands, as the staves of a barrel are held together with iron hoops; and to make a spread of empire on paper, Great Britain claims jurisdiction underneath the Aurora Borealis even to the North Pole, not yet visited.

Well, as France still retains St. Pierre and Miquelon Islands, near Newfoundland, notwithstanding that Canada was confirmed to Great Britain by treaty, signed in 1763, so Great Britain might retain the Queen Charlotte Islands, in the Pacific Ocean, north of Vancouver Island, after the temporary boundary fence from Lake Superior to the Pacific Ocean, and from 54°40′ to Demarkation Point in Beaufort Bay, shall have been modified into a partition with communicating doors between compartments, for Alaska the Russian-born Territory, and its neighbors also adopted into the Union family.

As Eastern Texas has prospered on cotton, so may Southern Manitoba prosper on wheat; but the development of Texas succeeded its admission into the Union, and Manitoba must ask to come in, and get in like Texas did, before it can attract immigration as Minnesota and Dakota do, alongside Manitoba, but inside the Union.

Serlick, on Red River, where the Canada Pacific Railway crosses and the Pembina branch begins, Moorhead, on Red River, where the Northern Pacific Railroad crosses, Omaha, on the Missouri River, where the Union Pacific Railroad technically ends, and Galveston, the principal seaport of Texas, distinguished for its export of cotton bales, are all on or near the same degree of longitude. Omaha, too, is midway between the mouth of Nelson River, in Hudson Bay, and the mouth of the Rio Grande, in the Gulf of Mexico. And the distance from Omaha to San Francisco is shorter than the distance from Omaha to Halifax.

From Port Moody, the terminus of the Canada Pacific Railway, on Burrard Inlet, mouth of Frazer River, to Port Nelson, Hudson Bay, the distance is shorter than from Port Nelson to Halifax. And as a harbor can be provided on a river emptying into Hudson Bay, if not on the Nelson, certainly on the Churchill River, then the trunk-line portage railway between the Pacific waters in or near Frazer River and a river port west of and accessible from Hudson Bay will, of course, be shortened correspondingly.

Consider a route from Europe to San Francisco, the Pacific States, and Asia, via Hudson Strait and Juan de Fuca Strait, with a portage railway between Frazer River and Hudson Bay, versus the Canada Pacific Railway via Ottawa to seawater and winter ice in the St. Lawrence.

The Hudson Bay Company throughout its long career sent its ships into Hudson Bay, and established numerous forts and fur factories on its shores. As to falls and cataracts in Manitoba, recall the condition of the St. Lawrence route between Port Colbourne and Montreal before the Welland and St. Lawrence Canals provided artificial navigation from Lake Erie and Lake Ontario to tidewater in Canada.

But whatever artificial works may be needed ought to be provided, to improve a river emptying into Hudson Bay, to facilitate the transhipment of commodities to and from Hudson Bay, which, in verity, is a sea, and the Pacific coast and intermediate points; and also to improve a river emptying into James Bay, or a harbor on James Bay, to facilitate the transhipment of commodities carried to and from the sea in James Bay and the Mississippi valley States; for where freight is bulky and weighty it is a consideration to shorten overland distance to tidewater navigation, because once on tidewater the way is open to destinations along the coast and across the ocean, by the cheapest known mode of transportation.

Meditate the tonnage between Chicago, Milwaukee and other lake ports and New York city, via the Erie Canal and the Hudson River tideway. Then count the meshes and the miles in the network of iron track from the Atlantic and Gulf ports from Galveston to Portland, inland and over the interior to cities on the lakes, from Oswego to Duluth. Lastly, extend this connected network, most of it of the standard 4 feet $8\frac{1}{2}$ inches gauge, northward to James Bay and Hudson Bay, and westward to the Pacific Ocean. Assuredly from Manitoba the outlook is broader and brighter southward and westward, than eastward via the Canada Pacific Railway, considered as a route to Montreal in summer, and to Halifax in winter, not to be intersected in Manitoba by cross-cut railway portages to Hudson Sea and James Bay!

The Canada Grand Trunk Railway, a rate-cutting competitor for Boston and Chicago traffic, in 1877 received per ton per mile, for freight carried, the average of only eight mills, or eight-tenths of one cent; and the travel over the Canada Grand Trunk, in 1877, averaged only fifty-eight passengers per train. Why? Because its revenue (profit unconsidered) would be still less than it is if its operations were restricted to the Dominion and Maine, and it had no ally in Vermont and Massachusetts.

And so, Manitoba, to prosper, must intertrade south as well as west; for with the eastern provinces of the Dominion it will have less intercourse and lighter intertrade than with the Western States of the Union, when its near-by bays, on which it abuts, shall have been made available for communication, via salt water, with the commercial world, in summer time.

CHAPTER V.

The treaty with Great Britain, signed at Washington May 8, 1871, for arbitration of the Alabama Claims, Fishery Question, the San Juan boundary, &c., a treaty in the negotiation of which Hamilton Fish, Secretary of State, was weighed, measured, and outwitted by his diplomatic adversary, and out of which grave mistake of President Grant's administration in forfeiting a "golden opportunity" has grown a grievance on the Fishery Question to be redressed hereafter, provides that:

"The navigation of the rivers Yukon, Porcupine, and Stikine, from, to and into the sea, shall forever remain free and open for the purposes of commerce, to the subjects of her Britannic Majesty and to the citizens of the United States."

The Porcupine River is a branch of the Yukon River, which empties into the Behring Sea north of the Aleutian peninsula, and the Stikine River empties into the Pacific Ocean in the vicinity of Sitka.

When Hamilton Fish, Secretary of State, in 1871, made the rivers of Alaska "free and open" to British subjects, why did he not stipulate that Frazer River in British Columbia, and the Red River of the North, and Lake Winnipeg and the rivers to it from the west, and the river from it to Hudson Bay, should be "free and open" to citizens of the United States?

The omission of the Red River of the North, which is four parts in Minnesota to one part in Manitoba, is extraordinary; and to suppose a blunder equivalent to it, one must imagine Austria, which pours its waters into the Danube, far above its mouths, omitted from treaties regulating its navigation to the Black Sea!

Hudson Bay is Middle Sea, and Minnesota and Dakota stand to it, via the Red River of the North, which empties into it under another name that does not change its nature or its course, as Austria and Servia stand to the Black Sea via the Danube, which has different names for its several mouths.

President Grant's administration had a national grievance proved against Great Britain, and reparation or war was the alternative; and yet Secretary Fish, in a negotiation to prescribe the measure and method of satisfaction—keep this in mind—permitted the insidious and ever-scheming enemy of his country (that aided rebellion in underhand ways and promoted piracy with English-built Alabamas, till American ships were almost swept from the seas and Great Britain became the monopolist of the ocean-carrying trade) to arbitrate, that is, to liquidate an injury to the United States which continues to inure to the advantage of Great Britain through its ocean ships, with a money consideration to be ascertained by a throw of dice or shuffle of cards—for what is arbitration but a game of chance, especially where a majority of the commissioners owe their nomination to foreign powers?

True, the San Juan Island arbitration resulted in favor of the United States by the decision of Frederick William I., Emperor of Germany, October 21, 1872. But the British claim to the island of San Juan under a forced interpretation of the treaty of June 15, 1846, was an act of British finesse and attempted bluff, to which the fitting answer would have been a notice that, after a date given, joint military occupation should cease, and that thereafter the army of the United States would occupy San Juan Island.

How the British intrigued at Berlin in 1872, and how Emperor William was beset to decide in favor of Great Britain, is matter of history. And it is to the impartiality of Emperor William of Germany, not to the diplomacy of Hamilton Fish, that the people of the United States are indebted for the possession of the strategic island of San Juan, acquired by treaty dated June 15, 1846, imperilled by arbitration authorized by treaty dated May 8, 1871.

The Halifax Fishery award, however, of $5,500,000, made November 22, 1877, by Maurice Delfosse, Belgian Minister at Washington, and Alexander T. Galt, appointee of her Britannic Majesty, for fishing privileges only worth a license to fish, not a ransom for fish caught in the saltwater highway—as brigands ransom tourists captured on the stage-travelled highways in Italy and Greece—will doubtless put a quietus on the international arbitration humbug, as between America and Europe. Ensign H. Kellogg was Commissioner for the United States, outvoted at Halifax.

The Congress of Vienna, 1814-15, distributed European territory and population, and exercised other powers, with as little remorse and not more penitence than a banditti distributes its spoils, made up of the proceeds of rapine on the highway and hearthstone.

France was prostrated and exhausted, a Bourbon was on its throne, and Napoleon had met his fate at Waterloo; so there was no military Satan abroad to make Europe afraid; but that very fact, for which diplomacy should have been thankful, made dynastic parties greedy, covetous and cruel. The Vienna Congress served the devil best, and set portions of Europe back (not including Austria and England) a period of time equivalent to two generations of men. And diplomacy did that fell work when war was at an end.

Turn, too, to the 1878 Congress of Berlin. The infidel Turk invaded Christian Europe and captured Adrianople in 1361, Constantinople in 1453. Turkish rule in Europe has been an outrage on humanity, christianized, through centuries of time; at irregular intervals the barbarities inflicted on the Christian subjects of the Porte have made their fellow-Christians shudder in all lands. And whatever was done to make Turkey relax her grasp on the Christian's rights in Europe, is mainly due to Russia. But for Russia the alternative would have been Islamism or massacre long ago.

After such atrocities as had never been surpassed anywhere (not even by the British in India, when, on the suppression of the mutiny of 1857, human bodies were discharged from the cannon's mouth), Russia, the chief champion of the Christian populations in the Provinces of Turkey, declared war against Turkey on the 24th of April, 1877. This war England could have averted by coöperation with the other signatory powers to the Paris treaty of March 30, 1856, but England, "perfidious Albion," refused. The treaty of San Stefano, dated February 19, 1878, inside of ten months from the declaration of war, attests the triumph of the Russian arms, for the Russian forces fought their way across the Balkans through the rigors of winter, occupied Adrianople, and at San Stefano were at the very gates of Constantinople.

And then it was, after the Turk has been whipped, that British bluster broke out; the British fleet of iron-clads, in violation of the treaty of Paris, and against the remonstrance of Turkey, steamed up the Dardanelles; the Parliament of Great Britain voted money, ostensibly for military and naval preparations, with a percentage for subsidy understood; for official servitors of impecunious dynasties include cheap human chattels, and as a little fuel will raise steam to blow a whistle, so will a few dollars raise wind to make a noise.

A scrap-book made up of official British correspondence and cuttings from the London newspapers, beginning with the Berlin Memorandum dated May, 1876, which Great Britain refused to sign, and which would have averted the war so disastrous to Turkey, by constraining that doomed despotism to grant the concessions asked for by the continental powers, would illustrate how the British lion was made rampant with imitation anger, till it swallowed an island belonging to its ally, and so with Cyprus appeased its hunger; for when British hunger is appeased, British pride is satisfied.

On the 13th June, 1878, a Congress of seven powers—Russia, Turkey, Italy, France, Austria, Germany and Great Britain—met at Berlin to discuss the treaty of San Stefano and preserve the peace with diplomatic chess; for secret societies and attempted assassinations had begotten a common dread that a general war might develop a new danger in social and political elements, antagonistic to the ruling powers represented by the Berlin plenipotentiaries, and which might in some places profit by war to promote revolution; since, however powerful a potentate may seem, he must have his people on his side, and must conform to public opinion in his action, to assure stability and justify succession in his line. Moral responsibility is inherited at every birth and pervades every life; and possession and power are identical only where the ruler and the ruled are cordial in coöperation. Hence ministers are slow to abet war where the people are not in accord with the aims of the administration in office, whether its chief wears a crown or holds a certificate of election; unless, indeed, where a man commands confidence from belief in his patriotism and greatness, and even then if he fall short he will fall far, for the nation is paramount and the individual must succumb.

On the 13th July, 1878, after a session of one month, the Berlin Congress signed a treaty and adjourned. If it did much, it left more undone, for its articles are only temporary trestles where arches of enduring masonry are necessary in a permanent way over a crisis which will periodically reappear, till the Turk return to Asia, whence he came to curse Europe with his false religion and his beastly vices.

In the Congress of Berlin the course of the ambassador of France is incomprehensible, save on the hypothesis that, because France under the first Napoleon sought to embarrass and thwart Alexander the First, till Moscow consumed his ambitious hopes of colossal empire in its ashes, and made him a fugitive from Russia, where his army left its bones in evidence of its destruction, therefore: France, wrong after the interview of 25th June, 1807, on the raft in the Niemen at Tilsit and the occult treaty of Tilsit of 8th July, 1807, wrong in the Crimean war of 1854–56, which was conceived and waged to make Russia a Baltic state like Sweden, must, to be true to its Russophobic wrong-doing, commit a final blunder at Berlin in 1878; where, after having voted against Russia and with England, it was made wise, when too late, with the information that meantime Great Britain was pettifogging and shystering for the Turk at Berlin, to play its high moral part in the European drama, it had negotiated a secret treaty with Turkey for its own aggrandizement in the Mediterranean, geographically in Asia, it is true, but politically and commercially, and in a naval and military sense, in Europe; in a place, too, where Cyprus under the British flag is a defiance to France, to say nothing of Italy and Spain.

In its foreign diplomacy, in which France was preëminent before the Buonapartes, France, since its seduction by Great Britain, has obviously declined; and among Britons and pro-Britons it is an opinion expressed with satisfaction that France has culminated in European politics, which is understood to imply that France is in its decadence; an erroneous opinion, which the Republic, when it ceases to repeat old history, and makes new history for Europe and mankind, will take care to eradicate.

Great Britain distrusts both France and Germany, because Great Britain knows and foresees that Belgium and Holland would be valuable acquisitions to France and Germany, inasmuch as they contain available harbors on the English Channel and North Sea, which in French and German ownership, by partition, would give prestige to French and German commerce in the waters of the world.

As to the *morale* of European politics—not as professed and propagated in debates and newspapers in Great Britain, but as practiced by Great Britain in its foreign affairs—it will suffice here to quote the reported words of Lord Derby in the House of Lords on the 18th July, 1878, after Lord Beaconsfield, on his first appearance fresh from the Berlin Congress adjourned, had made his statement:

"Lord Derby generally approved of what had been done in Europe, "but he questioned the value of Cyprus, and declared that he quitted "the cabinet because he dissented from the decision to seize a naval "station in the eastern Mediterranean, consisting of Cyprus and a "point on the main land, by a secret expedition from India, without "the consent of the Sultan."

Great Britain's role, as the ally of Turkey, was to coöperate with Turkey against mutual enemies, and to cheat Turkey for British private account. But the official Turk, first soundly thrashed by the Russian, and secondly bribed or biased by the Briton, was too thoroughly demoralized to stand on the San Stefano treaty, in which he was one of two negotiating parties, or to say "no" to an ally which bears and wears the prefix "perfidious" to its "Albion."

Every impartial observer the world over can foresee that the great power of the north, giant Russia, will never cease its efforts till the Bosphorus and the Dardanelles are so held and controlled that Russia shall have free and unrestricted passage for its commerce through the straits between the Black Sea and the Mediterranean, as Great Britain has for its commerce through the Strait of Gibraltar between the Mediterranean Sea and the Atlantic Ocean.

The Mediterranean Sea is to Russia precisely what the Gulf of Mexico is to the Mississippi valley. The Baltic Sea is closed by ice to navigation in winter, like the American lakes and the Hudson and St. Lawrence Rivers; but the straits to the Mediterranean are open throughout the year, like the Mississippi to the Gulf. And as the first Napoleon through his Moscow campaign, and the third Napoleon through his Crimean campaign, both failed to drive Russia back from the Black Sea towards the Baltic, the "manifest destiny" of Russia, in the providence of nations, should have made France in 1878 wise to prefer the Russians on the Bosphorus and in Constantinople, to increase of British jurisdiction in the Mediterranean basin.

Spain, France, Italy, Austria and Russia are the five principal powers which have common interests in Mediterranean navigation, whereas Great Britain's interests are mainly in India, and her ambition is to dominate the Mediterranean to protect her preferred route to the East. France built the Suez Canal across Egypt against the opposition and misrepresentation of Great Britain, but subsequently France allowed England to acquire part ownership of the Suez Canal. And this present year France, in shortsightedness akin to blindness, and as if in remembrance of Moscow and forgetfulness of Waterloo, coöperated against Russia in a way that aggrandized Austria and Great Britain, the two powers which in the Congress of Vienna, sixty-four years ago, impoverished and humiliated France to aggrandize and exalt themselves.

But the Berlin Congress is over, and to the shame of France, which returned home from the Congress of Berlin empty-handed, if not a dupe, Great Britain has added Cyprus to its Malta and Gibraltar fortifications for its army and navy in the Mediterranean (a Berlin Congress made *British Lake*), where France, Italy, and Spain ought to be absolute, but are not; and where, too, had France and Italy at Berlin been wise, they might always have Russia for a safe and sure ally, which Great Britain never is, by reason of its shifting policy of expediency and interest; because the Black Sea is no more than an affluent of the Mediterranean Sea, whence the Atlantic Ocean is reached, as Lake Superior is but an affluent of Lake Erie, whence the Atlantic Ocean is reached; and because, also, Russia at Constantinople could protect the waterway to the ocean-world.

The Black Sea and its tributary rivers, which pass their waters through the straits via Constantinople, are all within the hydrographic basin of the Mediterranean Sea, as the Ohio and Missouri Valleys are within the hydrographic basin of the Mississippi River; and Constantinople is to Odessa what New Orleans is to St. Louis; for St. Louis can only reach the ocean by natural waterway via New Orleans, and Odessa can only reach the ocean by natural waterway via Constantinople. And Russia at Constantinople would be no more a menace to the Mediterranean powers than is the American Union on the Gulf of Mexico a menace to the West India Islands. The Russian programme, which Great Britain has magnified into a pandora box to poison the Mediterranean air with suspicions, in truth makes Russia not the threatening enemy but the natural ally of the

Mediterranean powers, comprising France, Italy, Spain, and Greece; Great Britain, the task-master of India, not included:

To regain Gibraltar is a legitimate aspiration in a heroic Spaniard, and Spain has a history to beget patriotism and arouse ambition. And what better political purpose Spain can urge than the retrocession of Gibraltar, is past our comprehension.

To guardian the Suez Canal is a legitimate French ambition, for France promoted the Suez Canal when Great Britain underrated it, and disparaged and opposed it. Over Egypt, too, France should have retained the control it had when the Suez Canal was opened, under its auspices and through its material aid, and when Great Britain was in the background, wondering if the prodigal Khedive would soon sell or hypothecate his Suez Canal shares. In truth, France, had it been less jealous of Russia and more suspicious of Great Britain, might have sustained its appropriate role as the chief Mediterranean power, instead of surrendering to Great Britain that proud distinction, wrested from France by diplomacy that overreaches and by intrigue that undermines.

But the friends of the Republic of France need not despair nor despond, for its diplomacy may be revived and its prestige restored, under a progressive President elected by popular vote or its equivalent, as in the United States.

Possibly Great Britain may strive to anticipate France and make itself the ally of Russia, for Great Britain is a money power and its "interests" are chameleon in colors. But Russia has aims in Asia, and can there cause Great Britain tribulation, and so France and Italy may yet with Russia consult the "sick man" on his *straits*.

What Russia proposed to Great Britain anterior to the Crimean war is of record in official correspondence; and the acquisition of Cyprus Island by Great Britain is a testimony of the foresight of the Emperor Nicholas, as the fate of the first Napoleon is an evidence that the alliance proffered to France by Alexander the First would have spared France disaster in the field and loss in treasure and life. But the ways of diplomacy are "past finding out" in advance, though after events bear the marks of its visitation in scars impossible of misinterpretation. For is not the bomb of celestial fire a convincing proof when it explodes that electricity is a force in nature?

Is not Turkey shattered where riven by the Russian bolts of war in European Turkey and Asia Minor? Is not Turkey shorn of the island of Cyprus by its defensive treaty with Great Britain, signed June 4, 1878, whereby the latter stipulates to assist Turkey "if any attempt shall be made in future time by Russia to take possession of any further territories of his Imperial Majesty the Sultan, in Asia"—

not in Europe, be it noted and observed? And is not Turkey also shorn of Bosnia and Herzegovina by the treaty of Berlin, signed July 13, 1878, which prescribed that the two provinces named shall be occupied and administered by Austria? Is not the evidence conclusive that Great Britain and Austria coöperated against Russia, after its victories in war and its San Stefano peace treaty, to aggrandize themselves at the expense of Turkey? An orchardist anxious to save a tree stripped of some of its branches by a storm in an angry wind, does not cut off its remaining sound limbs. And yet, Austria and Great Britain, after the tree of Turkey had been trimmed with Russia's sword, from its top limbs to the ground, lopped off Bosnia, Herzegovina, and Cyprus, leaving the tree of Turkey like a weeping willow, with branches broken off by a tempest and limbs cut away with the axe—the first a consequence of war in the field, the latter of craft in the council.

Dynasties are not governments, crowned heads are not nationalities. Public opinion, founded not in prejudice or passion, but in conclusions based on reason, is the paramount power. And a dynasty that forfeits the confidence of the people it reigns over may be cast overboard without injury to the state, as a dead marine may be cast overboard by an admiral without injury to his fleet. Is not the Queen of England an ornamental feather in the scales that weigh political power in Great Britain? Did not the people of France, through their deputies in the Assembly, make it palpable to an equivocal Republican President and to Buonapartists in 1877 that the *coup d'etat* of December 2, 1851, is not possible a second time? And if in past time the voice of the people was smothered in superstition and ignorance by craft and chicanery, in present time "the voice of the people is the voice of God," in verity and earthly power.

The people of France and the people of Italy know and realize that their ambassadors to the Berlin Congress of 1878 were as clay in the hands of the potters who manipulated that conclave of jugglers, who adjourned grave questions and settled only minor matters.

In the Congress of Berlin the British ambassador, a lord by patent, sat with a secret treaty with Turkey in his pocket. In a congress of boys, a boy ambassador detected with a secret treaty in his pocket under similar circumstances would have been evicted for turpitude and disgraced among boys. But the Russian-Turkish war of 1877–78 is of record, and the San Stefano treaty is a historical milestone in the road from Moscow to Constantinople, Russia's ultimate destination, to which she directed her aims when the Black Sea was a Turkish lake, and the Crimea Turkish territory, as the American Republic looked hopefully and expectantly down the Mississippi River to the

Gulf of Mexico, when Louisiana belonged to France and Florida to Spain. Happily for the United States only one foreign power, Great Britain, was jealous of its acquisitions. But unhappily for Russia, which is a creditor nation by great odds in its account with other nations of help rendered and received, it has enemies and jealous neighbors who begrudge it what it wins, and plot to withhold from it what it deserves and will work on to achieve, for the betterment of Christian Europe.

Notwithstanding the jealousy of its enemies and neighbors, however, Russia, by the San Stefano treaty of 1878, even as modified by the Berlin Congress, changed the map of Europe; for it made Servia, Montenegro, and Roumania independent nationalities. True, Roumania showed its unworthiness of independence by its baseness to its benefactor; but nevertheless, Roumania is wrested finally from Turkey, and if portioned away hereafter so much the better, for on its inhabitants is imposed an imported prince impotent to prevent the retrocession of Bessarabia to Russia, or block the Russian's way to Constantinople. Servia is a national nut which diplomacy cannot crack to divide its kernel; and Montenegro is a star state, not a mould candle to be extinguished with Austrian or British snuffers. In a word, there are Christian fruits of wars past and germinating seeds of wars to come, on the Black, the Ægean, the Adriatic, and the Mediterranean Seas, which will restore to Christian rule its ancient sites, and make the Mediterranean a distributing basin under rights common to all the nations that have possessions within it, from Gibraltar to Odessa and the forks of the Danube.

CHAPTER VI.

In the Berlin Congress, which met June 13th, and adjourned July 13, 1878—a Congress wherein Italy and France fell short of the opportunity and the occasion—Russia did not have the hearty coöperation of a single power to assist it to maintain the concessions to the Christians it had won in war and secured by treaty. On the contrary, the powers present appeared to make common cause to harass Russia to the limit imposed by that victor on its capacity for endurance, to preserve the peace of Europe; for a war that, at its outbreak, would include Russia, Turkey, Great Britain, Austria, Servia, Montenegro and Roumania, would soon involve Italy and Greece and Germany and France, and so become general throughout Europe, where the embers of revolution were aglow, ready to blaze, in the summer of 1878. And against oppressed peoples roused to arms, the network of dynastic government is but as a spider-web. Peoples in anger are forces in nature, resistless as lightning, hurricane and flood.

Nor was Great Britain, with all its diplomatic brag and newspaper bluster, its parliamentary buncombe and its noisy preparation for war, including its dramatic transport of troops from India to Malta—a movement which included a hint to Italy and France—anxious for actual hostilities; because British ships in the carrying trade around the world would have afforded fat prizes to fast-going Alabamas incorporated into the Russian navy; for, clear as blue sky at noon-time, in sunshine, is the fact that, in a war between Russia and Great Britain, Russian ships of the Alabama style will scour the seas and make prizes of merchant ships. Great Britain breaks treaties and ignores treaties; and, as "curses come home to roost," Great Britain will suffer the consequence of her own practice, when she plotted the destruction of American commerce, with English-built Alabamas, manned with English crews, to prey on the commerce of the United States. England's aim was to sever the American Union, make a commercial ally of the cotton Confederacy, and strip the North of its ships on the seas, so that England could command the ocean-carrying trade of both sections. In the war of the Rebellion, England—abolition England—cared as little for the fact that human slavery, against which it had long kept up a loud outcry, was the basis of the Southern Confederacy it gave aid to in every conceivable surreptitious way, as England, in the war between Russia and Turkey, cared for the fact that the issue involved Christian emancipation from Mahometan servitude. At Berlin, Great Britain intrigued to divide the Bulgaria created by the treaty of San Stefano, so that Turkey might receive back Christian subjects released from its rule by Russia, and thereby prolong its stay in Europe, where it is a trespasser.

Great Britain has party cries, but no political principles. In its coöperative sympathy with the Southern Confederacy it forswore its moral convictions against human slavery and belied its loud-mouthed professions of philanthropy for the African in bondage. In its zeal for Turkey, so that for service in Bulgaria it might take pay in Cyprus, Great Britain, at Berlin, plotted and intrigued against the followers of Christ, in Bulgaria, to delay their deliverance from the followers of Mahomet, in Constantinople!

On the stage an actor can change his part according as he may be cast—in one play a patriot, in another play an apostate—because it is his profession to "hold the mirror up to nature" in his *imitations* of the characters in his text, from night to night. But nations are aggregations of individuals, and character does not consist of words spoken of a man, for that is reputation—a thing of newspaper manufacture—but is the product of a life, public and private. Character is pure metal, whereas reputation may be made up of alloys that swell size, but do not augment value. Thus, when, for illustration, the London *Times* says so and so of a British politician, its praise exalts and its censure depreciates reputation; but it does not affect character, for that is made up not of words, which are wind, but of deeds, which are weights and measures. Hence, Great Britain, long ago called "Perfidious Albion," is perfidious still, because, whilst it professes moral principles, it plays unworthy tricks for shop-keeper and money-lender ends. In the drama of progress, in the interest of civilization, in the last hundred years, Great Britain is immeasurably behind Russia; for Russia is not a rover, seizing here and there, but a progressionist, that pushes out its frontiers in the domains of anti-Christ, to spread civilization and develop the industries and the arts. Hence, Russia is a growing power, with a destiny to fulfill, whereas Great Britain is a moneyed power that makes the credit side of its profit and loss account paramount to its moral principles and religious professions. Russia abolished serfage, and will make other reforms as bold, after it secures peace on lasting terms.

Great Britain had opportunity to succor Turkey as an ally and co-belligerent, when Plevna surrendered and before the Russians had crossed the Balkans; and prior to the Russian occupation of Sophia and Adrianople, British and Austrian coöperation might have checked the progress of Russia, and so preserved Turkey nominally intact in Europe, leaving it to make concessions only to public opinion in matters of administration, without surrender of territory; for, rather than see the Christian Greek Church re-established in Constantinople, Catholic Austria and Protestant England would plot against Russia, and repeat the treachery of Judas to Jesus Christ. The over-fed priest-politician and the over-paid rector-politician are unworthy followers of the Saviour and His apostles; for, with the politician in robes it is self, self, self, whereas with the apostles it was everything for the cause of the Son of God on the earth, in a kingdom founded in unselfish sacrifice for the common good of mankind.

But Great Britain, the miscellaneous money-lender, whether for account of heaven or hell, and the promiscuous dealer in the necessaries of life and the poisons of illicit commerce, let perish the opportunity which tarried at Plevna and invited interference; and, in selfishness, looked on the sanguinary strife till Turkey was crushed and the San Stefano treaty had made peace between the belligerents. And by the San Stefano treaty between Russia and Turkey, the independence of Servia (God bless Servia!) and Montenegro (God bless Montenegro!), and Roumania the treacherous, was secured; and these three new independent nationalities were, by the Russian-Turkey treaty of San Stefano, added to the European powers. Bulgaria, too, after long suffering in servitude, was made an embryo nationality, with enlarged boundaries and a comprehensive programme.

The Berlin Congress, however, was called, and by that wire-worked conclave of wizards and dupes, the San Stefano treaty was revised, in common jealousy of Russia and in the special interest of Austria and England, because the ambassadors of Italy and France were unfit for their momentous missions—a fact which all intelligent and impartial Italian and French republicans feel and realize; and Austria, in exultation over Italy and France, occupies Bosnia and Herzegovina, and Great Britain, by a secret treaty, is in possession of the island of Cyprus, whereby its Mediterranean possessions are enlarged, and Italy and France are correspondingly belittled as Mediterranean powers. And thus meantime that the Turk—cruel to the Christians and treacherous to the Russians—was mulcted by the Austrians and Britons, Italy and France were treated as gulls, and appeased with words. Woe to the Berlin ambassadors of Italy and France!

What next may transpire in European Turkey is in the future, sealed from the knowledge of man. But that the Berlin treaty which ignored Italy and France as Mediterranean powers, aggrandized Austria and inflated Great Britain with bluster, is merely a postponement of a final settlement which the powers did not then dare to make, in the face of the socialistic and other agitations antagonistic to dynastic shams, frauds and pensions, is patent to every unofficial subject in Europe. Servia and Montenegro, however, both now independent— for the Berlin Congress did not venture to ignore the Servia and Montenegro provisions of the San Stefano treaty—occupy positions which justify expectations of aggrandizement. In truth, the theme of European Turkey bristles with possibilities which change shape according to circumstances, as sea waves take form and derive their force from the prevailing wind.

Russia and Turkey, as the two principals in the war, did their best, and Turkey made peace to keep the Russians out of Constantinople; for if the Porte had crossed the Bosphorus and fixed its head-quarters in Asia Minor, and a war of the powers had ensued, it is safe to predict that Turkish reign in European Turkey would have ended; though how the spoils might have been divided it is useless to consider.

However, with Turkey razeed into disproportion to Russia as a military power, Russia can contemplate the stay of the Turks in Constantinople as citizens of the United States contemplate the Spaniards in the island of Cuba. As a Spanish possession Cuba is not a menace; but the United States would not tolerate the transfer of Cuba to Great Britain, Germany or France. The Americans do not covet Cuba nor want it annexed to the Union, but the Americans would interpose to prevent the transfer of Cuba from the possession of Spain to a power rival or competitor to the United States; for with Spain the United States can cultivate reciprocal commercial relations, without danger of serious misunderstanding. And so, in like manner and from corresponding cause, Russia could contemplate Turkey, as left by the treaty of San Stefano, in possession of Constantinople, because Russia and Turkey could themselves carry out their own treaty and jointly regulate the navigation of the straits from the Black Sea to the Mediterranean. This reasoning, clear when the treaty of San Stefano was signed in February, 1878, is conclusive since the Berlin treaty of July, 1878.

True, the British, who have money to bribe corrupt men in office, and who wear brass to hide blushing, say that it is Russia which has been deprived of the fruits of conquest, waged for the deliverance of Christian populations from oppressions that darken history through generations of time; but the truth is, Turkey has been surgeoned where previously it had not been even singed; and to appease British lust, Christian emancipation has been indefinitely postponed, though Turkey is weaker if not smaller than it was left by the treaty of San Stefano; whereas Russia, with Bessarabia regained to the Danube and Pruth, and Batoum and Kars and about nine thousand square miles of contiguous territory annexed in Asia Minor, can recuperate in patience for another struggle when a propitious opportunity recurs; for Russia, vast and powerful as it is, cannot stay its march nor stop its wars whilst the Turk as an enemy patrols the Straits and lingers in Europe, a scandal to the Christian Church and a reproach to civilized mankind.

And perchance, whilst dynasties and churches plot and counterplot, the masses may exercise the inherent right of revolution, and make the crowned heads of Europe bend and bow down in the popular blast against tyranny and titles, like reeds and willows in a storm.

Russia Russianizes where it overruns, and the United States Americanize where they annex. France contains nothing but Frenchmen in a national sense, and all Germany is fatherland to Germans. Italy, too, is homogeneous, and Spain is a unit. But Austria is a cabinet-piece, stuck together with diplomatic glue, not a fusion of affiliating metals cast in a mould, as bronze is a fusion of copper and tin fluxed with zinc and lead to make it a limpid fluid for a casting satisfactory to the artist's eye and cohesive to withstand the weather.

Hungary is a seed-garden of discontent; and when the hydrographic basin of the Elbe shall have been made the model of a political potter's crock, Bohemia will be in Germany.

Lord Beaconsfield is Colonel Mulberry Sellers developed into Macbeth the ambitious, with his witches, only that his Duncan is in Constantinople and his witches are in India.

If a Cromwell were to rise in England, a Wallace in Scotland, and an Emmet in Ireland, and the labor organizations in Great Britain would simultaneously proclaim a Republic, the Houses of Lords and Commons would become the Senate and Assembly of a new Republic, and the British Islands would be United States, with a neighbor Republic in France, across the English Channel, and a sympathetic Republic in America, between the Atlantic and Pacific Oceans.

The case of R. A. Ammon, the brakeman, who successfully operated a railroad during the Pittsburgh riots in July, 1877, when mob rule prevailed in that city, where destruction was rampant from Saturday night to Sunday eve, under circumstances indelibly disgraceful to its military and police authorities and civic population, is an illustration of how an improvised administration, intuitively organized, might succeed in revolution organized out of riot, without disorder in civil administration. The people have only to organize their power with wisdom and apply it without rashness, to make revolution out of bondage into freedom a success in permanent reform.

And if this be deemed too hopeful a view of American adaptability or human intuition under free institutions which germinate ideas and expedients for exigencies unexpected and surprising, the example of General U. S. Grant should give peace to the doubting mind.

In May, 1861, U. S. Grant, a private citizen of Galena, Illinois, raised a company of volunteers in his own neighborhood, marched with it to Springfield, the capital of Illinois, and tendered his services to Governor Yates, who turned his constituent's experience to practical account in organizing the State troops; for U. S. Grant had served in the Mexican war, and was, moreover, a graduate of West Point, the national military school. Here, then, was material for a military schoolmaster, in a soldier trained and tried.

In time of peace he had retired to private life; but when secession appealed to the sword, he reappeared in behalf and defence of the Union; and how persistently and successfully he waged war and won battle is accepted truth in the familiar history of a pure patriot and great commander.

The unexampled cosmopolitan attentions paid U. S. Grant in foreign lands attest to a worldwide appreciation of his conspicuous merits, effulgent in fidelity and heroism to cause and country in civil war, and afterwards in good intentions in trying times.

From a private citizen U. S. Grant ascended step by step to the top-landing of commander-in-chief of all the armies of the United States; after a civil war of four years he was twice elected President of the United States; and on the expiration of his second term as Chief Magistrate, March 3, 1877, he again returned to private citizenship.

Honors are not titles, nor are titles merits. Deeds are finally only represented by names, and hence in after time, and to posterity, the name expresses all, is the symbol of everything. Wherefore Ulysses Simpson Grant, or otherwise and popularly and significantly United States Grant, stands for the whole subject full and complete, without abbreviation, reservation or contraction.

And when the European subject looks on the American citizen U. S. Grant, and sees in him an unassuming man without pretension and without title, surely the sight must suggest to his sober reflection the vanity of hereditary titles and the costliness of royal perquisites and pensions paid to the progeny of dynastic wedlock.

Grant rose out of the people, one of themselves, and, after public service in war and in peace, returned back to the people, one of themselves; and his example will be illustrious forever in a name aflame with patriotic fame; for in him is represented and embodied the trinity of duties only possible in a republic—private citizen, commander-in-chief, chief magistrate.

Those who advocate a third-term President would mar the finished picture of the man, for the third-term thought implies more than it expresses, and is not consonant with the precedent set by Washington and since observed as a law of sacred import, which cannot be misinterpreted to the American people.

When France welcomed liberty back to Paris, and drove the red-handed and incendiary torch-bearing communists from her temple desecrated by their diabolism, and for the third time consecrated the sacred edifice whose altar-fires had been twice before extinguished, France achieved a grand glory for army-ridden Europe.

To liberty in its dwelling-place in a republic a mob is a foe as dangerous and destitute of reason as a dog with the hydrophobia; for intelligent human beings prefer any and every form of government to anarchy; and as the bayonet as an instrument of order is the basis of despotism, as the ballot as an expression of power is the basis of republicanism, the enemies of order in free government are more than disturbers of the peace, and are to be treated, after notice reasonable to all not demons, like animals inoculated with the saliva of madness;

because between anarchy and order in a republic the law must prevail or liberty succumb to anarchy, the precursor to despotism; for trust breakers in office and charter-clad offenders who betray investors and wrong employés and transporters would barter away a state to a central authority for protection, and sell liberty to enjoy spoils; but where intelligent use is made of the ballot at the polls, abuses in the public service, in corporation practice, courts of law and elsewhere, can be reached and abated, and remedies provided for all evils curable by pure legislation and honest administration, from the chief justice to the street-sweeper. For as "the last shall be first and the first shall be last," so in a republic the bootblack-boy may rise above the chief justiceship to the presidency of the United States, and the born heir to fortune may die a beggar. The few make the noise, the many do the honest work of life; the tribunals try but a small percentage of the population for offences, and the jails are few and far apart, showing that fidelity to law and duty to society is the rule, disobedience to law and dishonesty to fellow man the exception; where there is ventilation in the newspapers, a foul transaction smells farther than an orchard in blossom, yet the fruit ripens in its season, by which time the rotten aspirant is in disgrace; modest merit survives in exquisite memories in the affections and in the books, but corrupt selfishness, like an *ignis fatuus* in foul air over decaying matter in a morass, is a luminous exhalation that misleads and disappoints; the bad man is on a trap-door with a possible rope overhead, sure oblivion beneath his feet, except as he may serve for an admonition in the sermons of prison chaplains and moral instructors of youth. Apathy, too, is sometimes deadly to liberty, as sleep is sometimes death in a disguise that disarms suspicion. In a republic inanition in a citizen is a crime against society, which can protect itself from a lunatic by confining him in an infirmary, whereas the citizen who omits to discharge his moral responsibility under the civil code is protected against incarceration, because to personal freedom he has a natural right not forfeited to the statute; for, though mentally defunct to political duty, he is physically alive in the social condition; information and experience are knowledge and wisdom, and government is exalted and pure in proportion as the governed participate in public affairs and adjust official conduct to a standard that will bear scrutiny, satisfy conscience and command respect. The individual must be a creditor in his account with the community in which he is an atom, possibly a light; and in proportion as he shows a balance to his credit large or small will he be esteemed much or little in the circumference of the circle rippled by his proceedings; for status is a valuation put not on promise but on performance; and herein is a reason why a man in conspicuous office or position who misdirects its influences and misapplies its patronage and powers, out of office sinks out of sight, and after burial in the earth is lost in oblivion deep as a thousand years; having strayed into forbidden ways and practiced unworthy arts, his name is cast out of the vocabulary of his cotemporaries, his coadjutors reproach him to excuse themselves, and the public know him no more; and as a luminary falls, so will its satellite disappear out of the firmament of preferment, where its borrowed light is shed in baleful beams. A community of stockholders has twice as many eyes and ears as tongues, and sees and hears more than it says. The wicked vanity that underrates the constituency it abuses, and trusts fortune to prevent its conviction in the courts, is helpless and without defence in the tribunal of the people, where lawyers' words are vapors, and lies, like damp rockets, will not coruscate.

The Philadelphia soldiers of the Pennsylvania National Guard who were abandoned to the mob and multitude at Pittsburgh, Saturday night, July 21, 1877, under circumstances indescribably disgraceful to the local military and police authorities, and who, having successfully defended themselves throughout the night, in a Round House, whither they had been improperly ordered by Major General A. L. Pearson, of Pittsburgh, marched out of that city Sunday, July 22, 1877 (pursued by a mob of baser beasts than bulls in a herd, which mob fired all its shots from the rear, and so did deeds of murder on the holy day), afterwards returned to Pittsburgh with recruits arrived out from home and fellow-soldiers from the interior and border counties, and reoccupied the scene of riot; in order that Pittsburgh should see and know, and to make Pittsburgh feel and realize in the spectacle of its submission, that the law is paramount and the State supreme in every part of Pennsylvania.

Where the law is defied free government does not discuss the *cause* of outbreak against order, life or property. It restores peace, makes arrests, assesses damages, and considers a remedy for prevention. And the Union is so extensive, and its spread-out population of readers and thinkers is so well informed on events past and present, that a local demonstration, whether aggravated for political party purposes or for arson, pillage, and murder, is followed by instant preparation to occupy the scene of riot; yes, that is the word—*riot*—for insurrection is farther from the intentions of a Pennsylvanian than is a vigilance committee in time of disorder for redressment. And the arson and pillage-approving population of Pittsburgh, quiescent where the Sunday mob in the public streets assassinated four strangers of the Pennsylvania National Guard, sent to Pittsburgh from Philadelphia by the State officers in authority at Harrisburg, was meek and quiet (and contrite concerning damages), whilst the military possessed Pittsburgh and forced it to eat "humble pie," meantime that railway traffic was resumed and trains departed and arrived on schedule time.

When Governor J. F. Hartranft arrived out at Pittsburgh with Pennsylvania troops, R. A. Ammon, the brevetted brakeman, resigned; and then Pittsburgh had opportunity in leisure to meditate the consequences of its mob sympathies, its Saturday night treacheries, and its Sabbath-day depot fires and highway murder of strangers under orders, in the service of the Commonwealth.

The crater of a volcano in eruption is an insecure place against the lava, cinder and muddy matter cast up out of a "bottomless pit;" but the place of torment for sinners doomed, with its mayor in a paroxysm, its police in a frenzy, its mob cantankerous and contentious, and its stokers overhot from overwork at its fires, as described by painters in colors and poets in words, is a place of mercy compared with pandemonium Pittsburgh on that saturnalian Sunday, July 22, 1877.

Dyeing certain colors is a lost art; and lying, notwithstanding the antiquity of the practice, is still an imperfect disguise and a poor substitute, else the efforts of the willing wills and weak minds that attempted to mitigate the guilt of Pittsburgh by the manufacture of imitation truth in crooked afterthoughts would have had a less mortifying termination; but the charcoal in the pyres along the railway tracks was too black, and the blood of the soldiers shot from behind was too red on the stones, and the crime of Pittsburgh was too fully recorded in its own and other newspapers of the day and in after documents and reports, for *lie* distilled from fiction to wash out its stains. And so Pittsburgh, over its dress suit of smoke, has a surtout of bills for Allegheny County to pay. The "insurrection" plea was a false key to open the Sinking Fund of Pennsylvania, which contains assets coveted for damages payable for the property destroyed during the Pittsburgh riot in July, 1877, due not from the State but from Allegheny County. The Governor of Pennsylvania, however, is a vigilance committee of one, with the veto; and in 1870 Governor Geary, with a veto that exploded like a bombshell, saved the Sinking Fund of Pennsylvania from robbery. The people of Pennsylvania all know who is Governor, and hold that functionary responsible for all legislation, except bills passed over his veto. Deriving the veto power from the Constitution, he is expected to use it for cause, or pass out of office and disappear from political life. To assent that a riot was an "insurrection," to substitute the State for Allegheny County in the matter of damages, would sink the Governor out of sight. But before it can reach the Governor a bill must be passed by both branches of the Legislature. Allegheny County is liable, and its resources are ample, and that is enough for justice.

And thus will it be again, if that European transplant called "socialism" and "communism," both parasites in a republic, should rise in arms against the authorities in any city in the United States. When peace is disturbed the law is not palaver but process with force, and order is to be maintained at whatsoever cost to its enemies; application for military aid is a dernier resort, but where invoked for sufficient cause it ought to be used with discretion and made effective against disorder. Especially is the American Union the wrong field for the agrarian from abroad, because his certificate of naturalization, which is proof of his promotion to citizenship, is not a license to sow treason, seize property, or overturn the social system which is the product of civilization since the deluge. In a republic the state is the aggregate of all the people in it, held together by its laws, enacted by representatives chosen by ballot at the polls. The minority cannot enact new laws, but by discussion and appeal may make proselytes to its opinions, till it reverses positions with the opposition and becomes in turn the majority party; whereupon it may graft its measures on the statutes. Violence or intimidation, however, is not only not allowable but is punishable, and as law-breakers, life-takers, and property-wreckers incur punishment, so their abettors, for head and heart guiltiness, deserve more than reprobation. If a discontented adult could on option turn political surgeon and butcher the law, according to his interest or his hate, the hand that would smite the state would be lifted against life, and society would retrograde. And this consideration makes the demagogue an outlaw in manhood, for he knows the end to which his arts tend; but the domestic and imported mischief-makers are few, and mob outbreak like yellow fever is only an occasional visitation in malarious spots, here and there, in the Union; an uprising of wicked malcontents would provoke a concentration and explosion of opposition force that would disperse them to the four winds, as a dynamite blast scatters quarry stones in atoms through the air.

The world craves not a new religion, nor will it abandon itself to the moral darkness of irreligion. Christianity has done for mankind more than all other religions summed together; and if the Turk reign at Philippi where Paul preached, that is because in 1878 England had for its idol of popular worship the boastful "Disraeli," the Queen of England being "Empress of India," where there are 240,000,000 of Hindoos and Mahometans, against 31,857,338 Christian subjects in Great Britain and Ireland. England's temple is the shop and workshop, and England's God is the "almighty dollar," to which her homage is loyal, if selfish; England's religion is not Christ crucified, but interest money accrued and to accrue. On "British interests," expressed and reserved, hang all the Acts of Parliament, all the Proclamations of the Queen. For the world, England, through half a century, has been commercial broker and commission agent. But this business is now open to competition, and in commercial supremacy Great Britain is each year less absolute. Of course, as she "weakens in the knees," she becomes lustier in the lungs, to frighten capital where she cannot harm it. England is overpeopled and London is overgrown, considering its proximity to the land's end in England, Wales, and Scotland, which have these areas and populations, to wit:

	Square Miles.	Census.	Population.
England,	50,922	1871	21,495,131
Wales,	7,397	1871	1,217,135
Scotland,	31,324	1871	3,360,018
Total, Great Britain,	89,643		26,072,284
Ireland,	32,481	1871	5,411,416
Isle of Man and Channel Islands,	394	1871	144,638
Army, Navy, Merchant Seamen,		1871	229,000
Great Britain and Ireland,	122,518		31,857,338
New York,	47,156	1870	4,357,647
Connecticut,	4,674	1870	537,454
New York and Connecticut,	51,830		4,895,101

New York and Connecticut, which in joint area are larger than England, jointly contain but 22 per cent. of the population of England; so that England contains more than four times the joint population of New York and Connecticut, notwithstanding that New York State contains New York City, Brooklyn, Buffalo, Albany, Rochester, indeed eight of the fifty principal cities in the United States; and Connecticut contains New Haven and Hartford, two of the fifty principal cities in the United States.

	1841.	1851.	1861.	1871.
Population of Ireland,	8,175,124	6,515,794	5,764,543	5,411,416

The famine in Ireland, in 1847, caused by the failure of the crops of that year, particularly its food staple, the potato, is not an explanation of the steady decrease in population in each decade since 1841. Great Britain imports more than half the wheat consumed by its population; and, as the palmy days of its foreign trade are past, emigration from Great Britain will unquestionably increase and resident population diminish in England as in Ireland. Foreign trade is uncertain; and as Great Britain loses its industrial prestige and customers for its manufactures in foreign markets, will not London, which by the census of 1871 contained 3,251,804 of population, decline like other commercial centres that preceded it in Europe? London is too large to subsist on the home trade of an island in the ocean, not twice the size of Newfoundland. From London to Liverpool, by railway across England, the distance is 201 miles. From New York to San Francisco, across the United States, by railway, the distance is 3321 miles. Between the Atlantic and the Pacific seaports of the American Union there are three thousand miles of prolific interior country, sure to contain, in time not distant, two hundred millions of inhabitants. Here is a prospect for a home trade very different from the outlook from London and Liverpool. Venice and Genoa had a distant trade, and lost it. The glory of foreign empire has departed from Rome, yet Rome is the capital of Italy nationalized, and is grand in its ancient ruins. And although the glory of commercial dominion over a vast area will leave London, yet London will still be the capital of the island of Great Britain; and Macaulay's New Zealander, who will inevitably appear, may contemplate its ruins, and contrast its vastness in desolation with its illustrious predecessors that flourished, each a cynosure for a time, and then declined towards oblivion, but not into it; because the historical inventory of the ruins of cities abandoned to decay is a perennial entertainment to the antiquarian and the student, which latter comprises all the ages of man; for the wise are seldom young, and the cultivated man at three-score years is as zealous a student as the better boy at school. The male animal that is a baby, boy, and man, in succession, if endowed with more than average intellect, is a thinking and remembering machine, from the time he can con the alphabet till reason leaves his head or life abandons his body.

"The Mutual Admiration Society," made up of rich and prosperous Americans and titled and snobby Englishers, which was in full blast preparatory to the negotiation of the Washington treaty of May 8, 1871, that was to do much for mankind, and elevate human nature to a higher standard in this world, preliminary to a still higher one in the next, seems to have moved the unbelief of one observer of men and matters, who wrote the following letter, copied from a newspaper of November 15, 1876. Its date, April 10, 1871, it will be seen, is anterior to the Washington treaty, signed May 8, 1871; and its publication, November 15, 1876, it will also be noticed, is prior to the Halifax Fishery award, made November 23, 1877.

"ENGLISH TACTICS IN AMERICA.

APRIL 10, 1871.

"GEN. U. S. GRANT,
    "*President of the United States.*

"HONORED SIR:—Distinguished men in distinguishing office are beset with too many flatterers and hear too few truth-tellers. And yet, to rulers of men, facts are as indispensable as food.

"Your answer to General Buckner, in 1862, drew my attention to you, and enlisted my confidence and good wishes. Your military case, however, as you know, is made up in the record of the rise and fall of an unholy rebellion. And now, in the high office which is the people's reward for services rendered them in the field, in a crisis which put in jeopardy the aspirations of mankind, you are again on trial, this time as Civil Magistrate, charged with the administration of the affairs of a great nation.

"And now to the purpose of this letter, which is, to caution you to beware of British diplomacy, which, like all European diplomacy, literally translated, is simply *lying according to law!*

"The Dominion of Canada was conceived in hostility to the United States; and American statesmen owe it to their posterity to sunder the zone of British territory which flanks the Republic on the north, and has its termini in the far apart islands of Newfoundland and Vancouver.

"The treaty of the 15th June, 1846, between the United States and Great Britain, which surrendered an *opportunity* to abut our boundary against Russia, at 54°40′, to which line Polk and Buchanan avowed that our title was 'clear and unquestionable,' is a standing shame to American statesmanship. And the interpretation subsequently given to that treaty, by Great Britain, to cover the island of San Juan, is a lesson which should not be forgotten at this time.

"I have been in England, and do not much wonder at the temper of its waning ruling class towards the United States. Jealousy, envy, covetousness are feelings difficult of eradication. The United States are overshadowing the British Isles. England's power is faded on the continent, and she is in dread lest her hoarded wealth be molested.

"But instead of looking to Africa, Australia, etc., for new fields and new markets, she continually aims to clog and thwart what, to a comprehensive vision, is the 'manifest destiny' of these States.

"If Great Britain were driven out of American waters, the two nations could, thereafter, be brought into relations of genuine fraternity. And until that event takes place, or British rule be limited to territory east of Lake Superior, the American heart which may yearn to find in Great Britain a *Mother Country*, will continue to find instead a step-mother country given to officious intermeddling.

"British territory cannot be Americanized under British rule, as witness the animus of the indwellers of that strip of land between Niagara and Detroit Rivers, across which railroad companies send freights and passengers to and from New York and Michigan.

"The valleys of the Saskatchewan and Red Rivers will never be *Americanized* whilst under the jurisdiction of the Dominion, or any other British authority, even though, of necessity (not choice), the railroads which may traverse them be connected with the railroads of Minnesota.

"British jurisdiction fosters opposition to the United States, exactly as a long British border tempts and promotes smuggling *into* the United States.

"Diplomacy and policy, more than arms, made the *greatness* of Britain. By diplomacy and policy she will make a bad neighbor of the Dominion of Canada, even as she makes corrupt tools in the Washington lobby.

"Do not mistake me. I am not an enemy to Great Britain. On the contrary, I appreciate the bulwark she made herself against the reactionary revolutions and usurpations of the continent. Nevertheless, Great Britain must be made to 'accept the situation' in the New World, and to back out of the way of American expansion and progress.

"You, yourself, know full well that what Great Britain did during the rebellion, prolonged the rebellion; that her acts, alike of omission as of commission, disclosed an impatience to see the Union dissevered; that she did *cause* the disappearance of American shipping from the ocean carrying trade between American and foreign ports. You know, too, that, before the American public, Great Britain is under *indictment*. And now, finally, what the American people have a right to expect is, that British diplomatists shall not once more *humbug American politicians!*

"Seward's Alaska purchase and diplomatic expulsion of the French from Mexico will jointly perpetuate his statesmanship.

"What page in American history is more *important* than Jefferson's acquisition of Louisiana?

"Polk's administration acquired California—a most potential and momentous acquisition; but the treaty of the 15th June, 1846, with Great Britain, was the mill-stone which sunk into oblivion the good deeds of Polk's reign.

"Under the indictment found against Great Britain, in the early documents of your administration, newspaper opinions, in England, were expressed in deeper contrition than at present time. Then it was even suggested, here and there, in some of the newspapers, that in settlement of the Alabama claims British territory might be ceded to the United States.

"Latterly, however, expounders of English public opinion have grown less penitent; and in lieu of willingness to eat 'humble pie,' the British lion is pricked into effort to imitate the ominous growl of yore, when it roamed the jungle in India, and before it was made a meek denizen of the zoological garden in London."

As in present time the administration of Thomas Jefferson is universally commended throughout the Union for the acquisition of Louisiana, and the administration of James K. Polk is credited without stint for the annexation of Texas and the acquisition of California, so hereafter and in full measure of thankfulness will the administration of Andrew Johnson (W. H. Seward, Secretary of State) be praised for the acquisition of Alaska and the Aleutian Islands; whereby Russia and the United States clasped hands across Behring Strait, and the rover of the seas and squatter on islands where the owner is in poverty or the natives are defenceless is shut out from fortifying a Malta in the North Pacific Ocean.

The precedent furnished by Great Britain in the ruthless extinction of the Transvaal Republic in 1877, and the annexation of its territory to her possessions in Africa, would justify the United States, as against Great Britain, in converting the provinces of British Columbia and Manitoba into Territories and embryo States of the Union. And why should not Great Britain have the "ingredients" of her drugged "chalice" "commended to her own lips"?

CHAPTER VII.

Since the 4th July, 1776, when the thirteen colonies, all on Atlantic tidewater (New Hampshire the northernmost, Georgia the southernmost, Pennsylvania the "keystone"), resolved themselves into "free and independent States," marvellous events have transpired, tending to overturn dynasties, expose the sham of kingcraft, and ameliorate the condition of mankind, under ratified treaties and written constitutions.

The fiction of "the divine right of kings" has perished from the earth; hereditary subjects have wrung concessions from hereditary rulers; Europe has been rectified in places, remodelled in parts; Russia, developed into a colossal civilizing power, grows and spreads; Germany is moulded into a homogeneous empire; Italy is a compact and intact nationality. And France, the fore-front of the world's stage when nations were in the cast of actors, in the seven years since the German war, has shown wise humility in calm self-restraint; has elevated still higher than before the arts of peace; and meanwhile has evinced a trust in her own capabilities and resources, under circumstances and in ways that vindicate the Republic, raised up out of the ruins of the empire and the ashes of the commune, as the form of government best fitted for the French people, in this third generation of political revolution, furnace ordeal and fiery trial. The third Republic, which demolished the empire and destroyed the commune, its two enemies and adversaries, one on either side, now stands "a pillar of cloud by day and a pillar of fire by night;" and no despot can make it vanish nor demagogue make it dark.

True, the face of Europe is still freckled with Heligoland, Malta and Gibraltar, and with spot powers in court-plaster patches between Skager Rack and Dover Strait, and between the river Pruth and the Strait of Otranto. But considering how much has been compassed in the rectification of European boundaries in the last twenty years, the prospect is cheering that the time is not distant when Europe will be apportioned among less than half a score of nationalities all Christian, the Turk retired; and that then the nations of Europe will at last be wise enough to live in peace with each other, content to allow distant peoples to govern themselves, and leave intercontinental intertrade to regulations prescribed in treaties.

The time will soon have gone by for partitioning off the earth among dynasties supported sumptuously for breeding stock through royal marriages for diplomatic ends; in Europe nowadays nationalities command paramount consideration, and the reigning houses rule not by "divine right," but as the constituted and installed heads of the governments; for, after all, an empire is but another name for a state, and from an autocracy to a democracy the distance is but a bridge of spans on different plans, whatever may be said about constitutional monarchy, with a pensioned household and a class made noble by patent, as if a patent of nobility were a gauge of merit, when it is only evidence of a machine-made honor or a prize-ticket gift; for a patent cannot ennoble a name or make a name great, because true greatness is the homage paid by mankind to public benefactors for unselfish service; and it is with men as with books and battles, only one here and there serving to make a fame or mark an epoch or era in the chronology of time.

Great events in America, due to patriotic effort and self-denial, have wrought out grand results to universal man in a new nation and in the old world. The government of the United States has withstood attack from without and also from within, has had foreign wars and a civil war, and was strong enough to triumph in both ordeals. Slavery, the graft of Great Britain, has been extirpated, and now there is not a seed of poison in the Constitution to germinate a parasite or justify a reproach. And the corrupt lobbyist, bribe-taker and trust-betrayer, the corporation anaconda and the ring boa-constrictor, would fain rehabilitate as conservatives good as Tweed and his coadjutors, who, having amassed millions contrary to honesty and duty, if let alone and not molested or exposed, would advocate low taxes, civil service reform, economy in corporation practice, and dividends to stockholders. But the sword of justice is unsheathed, and offenders fear lest where it may not smite with its edge it may smack with its flat side. The uneasy sinner is the dishonest man found out. And for the hypocrite who delivers himself of his moral lecture from the chimney-top, and descends thence by the flue to emerge sooted from the cellar, or makes the editorial column or the official corporation report a vehicle for deceptive untruth, exposure is sure disgrace as contempt is sore punishment; because the offender who may indurate his face and banish the blush from his cheek cannot deaden the sensitive nerves between his five senses and his mental reflections.

For bankrupts in reputation look not alone among delinquent debtors in ordinary and unofficial transactions, but also to those who betrayed official trust, and after investigation or trial were hurled down from the pinnacle of high esteem into the dusty way where the tramp travels.

As a political coupling the Constitution is potential to hold together the train of States from Maine to California; and all the mending the Constitution needs is to make the presidential term six years instead of four, render the incumbent ineligible for re-election, and guard the franchise and the electoral return against fraud.

All attempts to found royalty in North America have failed, tragically and ignominiously. Mexico has had two emperors, Iturbide and Maximilian, whose short reigns are bloody chapters in its eventful history; the first-named was shot after a trial in 1824, the last-named was shot after a trial in 1867; and these two tearful lessons will not be lost on diplomatists, adventurers and demagogues.

The progress of population in the nation of the United States is without precedent, as will be seen in what follows.

The estimated number of inhabitants in the colonies represented in the Congress at Philadelphia in 1775 was 3,000,000.

At that time the colonies ranked in population Virginia first, Massachusetts second, Pennsylvania third, Maryland fourth. New York was equalled by Connecticut, North Carolina and South Carolina. Maryland contained 62,035 more of population than New York, and 62,034 less than Pennsylvania. The original colonies all abutted on tidewater, and among the three millions of population are included Tories who were averse to independence and non-combatants in love with peace.

The first census of the nation of the United States was taken in 1790, so that in all there have been nine decennial censuses, beginning with 1790 and including 1870. And here is the record made of the aggregate population at each census:

1790.	1800.	1810.	1820.	1830.	1840.	1850.	1860.	1870.
3,929,214	5,308,483	7,239,881	9,633,822	12,806,020	17,069,453	23,191,876	31,443,321	38,558,371

According to the ninth census of the United States, taken in 1870, there were of native-born inhabitants 32,901,142.

Foreign-born inhabitants 5,657,229.

The population of the United States, consequently, in 1870 comprised eighty-five per cent. of native-born and fifteen per cent. of foreign-born population.

Unfortunately America is a misnomer, as to call England Anglo-Saxon is a misnomer; for Christopher Columbus, not Americus Vespucius, discovered America, and England is Saxon-Norman, and America is Celtic-Teutonic. In proof of this, attention is invited to the nationalities of the foreign-born population of the United States in 1870.

Ireland,	.	1,855,827	Norway,	.	114,246	Mexico, .	.	42,435
All Germany,	.	1,690,533	Sweden,	.	97,332	Denmark,	.	30,107
England,	.	550,924	Switzerland,	.	75,153	Italy, .	.	17,157
All British America,	.	493,464	All Austria,	.	74,534	Belgium,	.	12,553
Scotland,	.	140,835	Wales,	.	74,533	West Indies,	.	11,570
France,	.	116,402	China,	.	63,042	Russia, .	.	4,644

The first battle of the revolution was fought at Lexington, Massachusetts, April 19, 1775. On the 19th October, 1781, Lord Cornwallis with his army surrendered to General Washington, at Yorktown, Virginia. Provisional Articles of Peace were signed November 30, 1782. An agreement that all hostilities should cease was signed January 20, 1783. On the 19th of April, 1783, exactly eight years after the battle at Lexington, which opened the war, a proclamation of peace was issued by Washington.

From the achievement of Independence the American Republic has been an attraction to immigrants, particularly from Ireland and Germany; and from these Celtic and Teutonic sources the Union has derived the bulk of its foreign, the basis of its native population. And as the issue of foreign parents are native Americans, and the process of fusion has been in operation since Europe peopled America's shores, the American race is a *Celtic-Teutonic*, not an Anglo-Saxon type of the human species. It was the Norman graft that made Britain great. And where the Normans grafted there they grew.

What happened to Adam and his posterity may be left to historians, prophets, and preachers to descant, for an initial in Noah and the ark-load which he landed on Ararat; since this brings us down to a period relatively modern, and gives the human family a new departure from Armenia, not far from Eden and all in Asia.

The Dominion of Canada, organized as a propaganda, cannot crown a ruler, install a dynasty, nor manufacture an aristocracy by patent-right; for exotic shoots from royal roots, or suckers from noble stumps, do not sprout after transplant to North America, where old States sow pioneers and new States grow from home increase and European overflow.

The Union is the product not of birthright but of honest industry, Christian toleration and educated self-reliance. The people reign and the people rule; and incumbents of conspicuous office, not conspicuous for merit, may flash in the political sky like a rocket in the night air, but are sure to disappear from public office, public consideration, and public sight. True, parasites abound in political life as in animal and vegetable life; but dishonesty begets opprobrium, and the unfaithful public servant sinks into obscurity and is heard of no more, save to "point a moral and adorn a tale." To be sure money will buy praise, but the promiscuous flatterer is like the fly which leaves a speck of dirt where it finds a grain of sugar.

The robust man is not always healthy in all his vital organs, but the tendency of nature is to health, and unless the wrong medicine is administered he soon recovers.

So the political body may not be perfect in all its parts, yet it may be complete in most of its functions, and only need repair where there is discovered imperfection. The duration of office is limited, and constitutions and laws are open to amendment. The bullet is the unthinking instrument of force, used against the subject if he claim the rights which it is the duty of the citizen to exercise. Man can nowhere be free but in a republic. And if the subject boast of the pure blood of his prince, the citizen can cite the purer blood of the race-horse, which receives a physical training superior to a prince in paternal antecedents and safeguards against indulgences and indiscretions.

As a large percentage of the patent medicines sold in the shops are quack nostrums, so a large percentage of patent title-bearers are spurious compounds, labelled to circulate at a social price above intrinsic value. And the divorce courts of Europe attest that tempted virtue is sometimes weak to resist vice as well where rank is acquired by inheritance in circles professedly exclusive as among less pretentious people.

England produced Shakspeare, America produced Washington. Neither of these men inherited a title, yet each left a fame that time brightens, as royalty dims, in the shadows of " coming events."

A living body, the planetary system, the universe of God, are all machines in motion, operating to the schedule of the Supreme intelligence, the Creator of the earth and of Adam in Eden, and all things between and beyond the outermost orbs in space, visible through the magnifying aids to science and research.

The astronomer contemplates the heavens and is filled with adoration of the Maker of the firmament. The statesman with his finger revolves a ball mapped with the nations of the world, and, contrasting the imperfect machinery of human government with the order in nature, applies himself to the improvement and aggrandizement of his country.

The nations of Europe, though the issue of a new departure out of Noah's ark in Armenia, after the deluge, are nevertheless a spread-out of patches cut with swords and held together with treaty tape; and in this patchwork of centuries every rent makes two "ragged edges," one of which is pieced out, the other cut away, as when Savoy and Nice were scissored from Italy and fitted to France, and Alsace and Lorraine were sworded from France and sewed to Germany.

Or later, as when the Berlin Congress in 1878 donated to Austria, for reasons not founded in truth nor of a justifying nature, the Turkish provinces of Bosnia and Herzegovina, for Austria did nothing whilst Russia and Turkey were at war, but chorus with Great Britain in bluster and preparation, not however, as the sequel shows, to fight Russia and risk an European conflagration, but to steal from Turkey in its extremity; because it was clear that Russia would not vacate Bessarabia, Batoum or Kars, having vanquished Turkey in war ended by the treaty of San Stefano between the two belligerents. And therefore, Great Britain and Austria negotiated and threatened in the interest of Turkey, against Russia and the San Stefano treaty, till the map of Turkey was rectified by the Berlin Congress, which portioned off Bosnia and Herzegovina to Austria, and Great Britain obtained Cyprus Island through a secret treaty.

Turkey's volunteer attorneys divided part of their client's assets between themselves, and then conciliated their plundered dupe with the excuse, that it had better part with Bosnia and Herzegovina to Austria and Cyprus Island to Great Britain, than carry out with Russia the provisions of the San Stefano treaty. And when the Berlin Congress prescribed for Austria's aggrandizement, its "mandate" was equivalent in dishonesty to a military order to billet troops in a bank to manipulate its affairs, lest thieves might break into its vaults and steal its deposits. It is because the diplomacy of Europe is operated in the interest of dynasties, sometimes in disregard of the populations governed, that extreme opinions are promulgated through secret societies, and imperial rulers live in political twilight and intellectual unrest.

In horse-power times gone by, the weight of a four-footed animal on a treadmill which turned under its feet propelled a boat across a ferry, and caused light machinery to move in a mill; but nowadays the steam-engine hauls trains of cars over mountains, propels ships across seas, and drives looms in factories. And as the steam-engine is a motor in machinery, so is the ballot a motor in government. The sceptre is no longer a magic wand; and the one-man power in a crown is falling into disuse after the one-horse power on the treadmill: for this is a practical age, and a wooden figure-head is an abomination in the sight of thinking man, who associates the idea with a vessel in water, where a figure-head does not interfere with the bowsprit nor impair the discipline of the crew on board.

Institutions influence the minds of men as climate affects crops in the ground. There must be an even start or there can be no fair race. To be born free and equal in the law is a stimulus to effort, and hence in a republic the honest, earnest man moves on even in the front, incurring risks and enjoying rewards.

The productions of an arable belt of land outstretching north and south across twenty degrees of latitude, say from Galveston in Texas to Pembina in Minnesota, are of very many more varieties than the productions of a belt due east and west across twenty-five degrees of longitude, say from Winnipeg to the Pacific waters, in the Dominion of Canada.

The better side of Manitoba is its south side, open to the sun and zephyr, which thaw its surface to its isothermal limit, and give it a season for agriculture. Manitoba will be forced by necessity to cultivate a trade southward, because the staples of which it may produce a surplus, over home consumption, will be very few; whereas the States south of Manitoba grow oats, grasses, rye, barley, potatoes and wheat; and also corn, flax, hemp, tobacco, rice, sugar cane and cotton; vegetables and fruits, too, are in boundless profusion.

In verity the capacity of the Mississippi basin for production is beyond estimate by ordinary calculation; for, though the earth is peopled over its circumference, one-third part of its inhabitants dwell in China proper, within an area but little larger than the Mississippi basin, and not so large as the joint area of the Mississippi basin and the thirteen original States; in other words, one-third of the whole human family dwell in less space than that portion of the Union which is east of the Rocky Mountains!

In 1871, England, within its area of 50,922 square miles (Minnesota is larger than England and Scotland together), contained 21,495,131 of population. And Great Britain and Ireland, comprising England, Wales, Scotland, Ireland, Isle of Man and Channel Islands, altogether 122,518 square miles (the area of Minnesota and Iowa, jointly, is 138,576 miles), in 1871 contained a population of 31,857,338. These sizes are suggestive, because in 1770, one hundred and one years prior to the census of 1871, England and Wales contained a joint population of only 7,428,000. In the beginning of the present century (1801), the population of "London and suburbs" was 864,845; in 1870 the population of New York city was 942,292, and, including its suburbs, about 1,750,000; so the United States, in 1870, contained a larger city than Europe contained in 1801, notwithstanding the antiquity of its capital cities and trade centres.

Philadelphia, too, is destined, from natural causes, to be a city of very large population; it is on a deep and broad tidal river, and is encircled by garden country of unequalled fertility; is in close proximity to mineral regions that supply cheap fuel and command the seaboard market; is a focus of communications to the sea, the lakes, the cotton States, the Mississippi basin, and the Pacific coast; finally, Philadelphia is a city of cheap homes and teeming markets, and its working population, skilled in an infinity of arts, prosecuted in establishments of all sizes, from ground plans that cover acres to an attic floor a few feet square, have opportunities for country recreation in its parks; for the education of children in its schools; and for the instruction and entertainment of everybody in its churches, libraries and public places.

Philadelphia contains but a comparatively small percentage of foreign-born, is intensely American in its political sentiments, and if less metropolitan in appearance and fashion than its neighbor, is more American in its proclivities and more multifarious in its manufactures. And fortunate is it for the whole country that the cities of New York and Philadelphia, and the States of New York and Pennsylvania, so near together in geography, are so different in characteristics and employments; for as "familiarity breeds contempt," so similarity breeds indifference, because "variety is the spice of life;" and so when New York and Philadelphia are considered together, their differences are bases for intercourse and intertrade, as the differences between two nations furnish groundwork for commercial treaties; since two nations that grow the same staples, manufacture the same things and deal in the same merchandise, have nothing to interchange, no ground for compromise, no plea for reciprocation. A nation that buys **outside of its borders must** sell outside of its borders, **else** treasure instead of flowing inward will be drained outward; but as no nation can supply all its own wants, every nation must buy in foreign markets; and these necessities are the true bases of international intertrade. Thus the United States is a buyer of coffee, tea and sugar, and a **seller** of cotton, breadstuffs, oil, and provisions; true, there are scores of other articles besides these in the catalogue **of the** foreign trade of the United States, but the articles named constitute the principal items in the import and export lists. Of the manufactures **of** iron, cotton and wool the United States import less and less from year to year; and herein is where the shoe pinches Great Britain, which covets the American market, and so preaches free trade **to** dissuade America from following in British footsteps through a **period** of protection, till its manufactures were established and its **labor** trained.

The native American and the **foreign-born** citizen both know and **appreciate** the condition of the subject in **Europe** too well to permit the lawyer-politician, or any one else in Congress, to vote away **protection to** American labor, not so much for the benefit of the British laborer **as** the British aristocrat, whose established *caste*, made up of dukes, marquises, earls, viscounts, barons, own the land and enjoy the luxuries of life.

The manufacturing plant now in operation in the United States is of so large capacity that the competition is sufficiently active between **the** home manipulators of our own staples; so free trade means oppression to the American laborer and loss of American capital invested in machinery, because in Great Britain labor is impotent for its own **protection** against the aristocracy which is above it, as a weather-vane **on** a church steeple is above its foundation-stone.

The Northern Pacific Railroad Company, in its general account, which has a total of $147,251,212 on $20,545,883 charged to construction and equipment, twice the money-cost of road built and equipped, has this item:

"**Assets** acquired under decree of court, $44,966,583."

These assets doubtless consist mainly of the par of shares or bonds mostly bonus, and not convertible into money at any price worthy of consideration. Yet the item has "millions in it"—in the books!

Great Britain undoubtedly is possessed of prodigious wealth, particularly if its investments at home and abroad be counted at par; but Great Britain is a small country, whilst its investments are in all parts of the earth, from which the principal of money loaned can never be recalled, for certificates of loan are cut out and off by foreclosure, sale and reorganization, and bankruptcy is a sponge that obliterates book accounts.

Great Britain, too, has a foreign trade which diminishes in profit; and so from its foreign investments and its foreign trade British income is reduced. Thus Great Britain is menaced with loss in its capital and in its trade.

The exceptionally favorable condition of the foreign trade of the United States in recent years will appear in the following exhibit of the imports and exports for the last four official years, compiled from reports of the Chief of the Bureau of Statistics:

Year ended June 30,	1875.	1876.	1877.	1878.
Domestic Exports—Merchandise reduced to gold values,	$499,284,100	$525,582,247	$589,670,224	$680,683,798
Domestic Specie,	83,857,129	50,038,691	43,134,738	27,054,985
Total Domestic Exports,	$583,141,229	$575,620,938	$632,804,962	$707,738,783
Foreign Exports—Merchandise,	$14,158,611	$14,802,424	$12,804,996	$14,200,402
" " Specie,	8,275,013	6,467,611	13,027,499	6,678,240
Total Foreign Exports,	22,433,624	21,270,035	25,832,495	20,878,642
Aggregate Exports,	$605,574,853	$596,890,973	$658,637,457	$728,617,425
Imports—Merchandise,	533,005,436	460,741,190	451,315,992	437,097,237
Imports—Specie,	20,900,717	15,936,681	40,774,414	29,821,313
Total Foreign Imports,	$553,906,153	$476,677,871	$492,090,406	$466,918,550
Summary.	1875.	1876.	1877.	1878.
Exports from the United States,	$605,574,853	$596,890,973	$658,637,457	$728,617,425
Imports into the United States,	553,906,153	476,677,871	492,090,406	466,918,550
Excess of Exports over Imports,	$51,668,700	$120,213,102	$166,547,051	$261,698,875

Here, in verity, is a progress to be proud of, for no other nation can approximate these relative proportions in export and import trade. The summarized result given demonstrates conclusively that the American Republic exports largely more than it imports; that the Americans sell to foreigners much more than they buy from foreigners; and that the Americans are a creditor people in account current with the intertrading nations of the earth. This, truly, is the acme of commercial superiority and independence.

The American Union is the largest producer of the precious metals, wherefore gold and silver must be added to its breadstuffs, cotton, oil, tobacco, provisions and manufactured articles, the miscellany being distinguished as well for its variety as for its value.

Since the rebellion against the Union, which was suppressed in 1865, after **four years of civil war**, the nation **of** the United States has **more than doubled its exports** of domestic merchandise to foreign countries; and since 1873, when inflation collapsed after six years of **rampant speculation caused not by** the war whereby the rebellion was suppressed, as erroneously alleged by quack political economists and artfully **charged by charter-clad** banditti, but by the Union Pacific **Railroad Company's Credit** Mobilier contract of 1867; Northern **Pacific and Texas Pacific, and** scores **of other railway swindles on investors of small savings;** the incorporation of roving contract and **improvement companies by the** Legislature of Pennsylvania, particu- **larly in 1869–70–71; and** kindred false pretences contrived to **cheat the people with** counterfeit **tokens** in the similitude of negotiable bonds. Never was history more cunningly perverted than **when it is made to charge to the war of** 1861–65 the lottery-policy railway bond and bonus railway share speculations of 1867–73. And high- **waymen and** brigands, who incur personal **hazard** in their out-door **depredations, are** heroic **thieves** contrasted **with an** equal number **of official sneaks clad** in **charters** granted for **public objects, but per- verted in practice to promote private ends in** dishonest ways.

The **government of the** United States **had resources** in custom duties, **taxes, etc., to pay interest** on its indebtedness; but corporations, firms, and **individuals as** debtors had to pay interest out of principal borrowed, where the **profits** earned were insufficient, or fail. And as **money borrowed was soon** expended or divided, and the profits were **less than the interest payable,** disaster was the inevitable conclusion under the circumstances.

The outlays charged to construction and collateral purposes **by corporations of all kinds,** managed by bonus financiers and by san- **guine men,** and by firms and individuals for new establishments **devoted** to the industries and manufactures, and for alterations and additions made to enlarge capacity and facilitate production, during **the six consecutive** years from 1867 to 1873, amounted to a prodigious aggregate of liabilities, bearing interest at a rate extra- ordinary in some cases and **high** on the average; whereas those who bought United States bonds during the war invested their own money, and consequently did not incur debt in the transaction. The war absorbed capital in United States bonds for investment, and to its creditors the **government** has been faithful in the payment of interest accrued; but in the six years of speculation (commencing two years after the war had ended, and after the government had not only ceased to borrow but had decreased the national debt and the annual interest payable by the United States), many more millions of indebtedness was rashly and recklessly incurred than the total interest-bearing debt of the United States, which, at its maximum, August 31, 1865, amounted to $2,381,530,294.

This is a large sum, it is true, charged against the United States; nevertheless it is not near so large as the charged *increase* in the liabilities of the railroad companies in the United States, from the end of 1867 to the end of 1873, as witness:

	1873.	1867.	Increase.
Miles of Railroad reported on,	66,237	30,000	36,237
Capital Stock,	$1,947,638,584	$756,223,000	$1,191,415,584
Funded Debt,	1,836,904,450	416,658,000	1,420,246,450
Total liabilities,	$3,784,543,034	$1,172,881,000	$2,611,662,034

If the entire railroad mileage in the United States had been reported on, and all the floating indebtedness included, the increase in the liabilities of the railroad companies for 1873 over 1867 would be about $3,000,000,000!

At the end of 1873 there were in operation in the United States, of railroad, 70,857 miles. Railroad constructed in six years ending **December 31, 1873,** in the United States, 31,508 miles, exceeding the total railroad mileage in the United States at the outbreak of the **rebellion** in 1861. Thus there were more miles of railroad built in **the United States in the six** years subsequent to 1867 than in the **thirty-five years prior to 1862!**

France prospered after the disastrous war of 1870–71, otherwise it could not have so promptly paid its enormous indemnity to Germany.

Great Britain has had no costly war for a long time, but Great **Britain** is depressed to extremity in its trade and industries, notwithstanding it has enjoyed a long peace.

Eight years elapsed **between** the end of civil war in the United States and **the financial crisis in** 1873. In a diagnosis of the United States the war which ended in the spring of 1865 is not the cause of the depression since the summer of 1873; on the contrary, the collapse of credit in 1873 was **caused** by speculation and expansion commenced **in the** summer **of** 1867, prior to **which** date Tweed's Tammany Ring, the Union Pacific Railroad Company's *Credit Mobilier* contract which surpassed Aladdin's magic lamp, the Southern Railway Security rover, the Northern Pacific Railroad bond bubble, the California and Texas Construction Company's Texas and Pacific Railway juggle, and kindred inventions of bonus financiers, **were not** in existence.

The capital of a nation **is its** principal in excess of its debts, and **a** nation is rich when its income from investments and its profits from its trade jointly exceed its interest payments and all outgoes chargeable to expenses. Where there **is** a balance to the credit of a year, the surplus of income over outgo is capital accumulated. But where **a nation expends more than** its receipts, it diminishes its capital or **incurs debt. And as Great** Britain in recent years has imported **many millions** more in money value than it has exported, and **has** collected **a diminished sum** from its foreign investments, the conclusion is **that in** recent years Great Britain has been living in part on its principal accumulated in prior years; for as a creditor Great Britain has incurred immense losses in foreign countries and corporations.

CHAPTER VIII.

In the spread of commerce nations achieved greatness and cities **amassed** wealth, which, **however,** neither could hold, and consequently, the commercial centre of the world, moved **from** place to place around the Mediterranean shore, and thence to the Netherlands, at last was shifted to the Thames, and London was developed **into a** vast city. But London cannot go on growing forever, and as its income, commissions and profits are now greatly reduced, compared with years gone by, London may at any time suffer from panic and from shrinkage in value of real **estate. And as the** exodus of skilled workmen from Great Britain is certain to continue, London will ere long feel and show the effect of decadence in principal invested and income collectable. **The** volume of business may be large, the measure of profit may be small; machinery superseded, property depreciated, markets divided, **competition aggressive;** these **are** the tendencies of the times in Great Britain, and these are the considerations that determine intelligent Britons to seek the United States, where, if the shops are full at present, there are cheap lands open to settlement. Interesting, instructive and consolatory is the migration to the agricultural lands west of the Mississippi River, already penetrated with **railways and** provided with transportation.

The Eastern States are all importers of agricultural products from the West; and, meanwhile, **as** the East grows in population, consumption will increase; and so the West, itself a large consumer of its own products, has a customer in the East, and beyond the Eastern States is Europe. For surplus populations accumulated in particular branches of industry, as labor is divided at present time, there is no such corrector and regulator as agriculture. In a short time, therefore, with proper duties on the products of foreign labor at starvation prices, the internal affairs of the United States will adjust themselves to a new distribution of domestic employment, and "all things will work together for the common good," like trains on a railroad, to a new time-table.

Chicago, a marvel of rapid growth, will continue to develop and increase in population, in manufactures and in trade; St. Louis likewise is sure of long continued commercial expansion and industrial accumulation; New Orleans will be the entrepot of prodigious totals of cosmopolitan commerce; and St. Paul will be conspicuous and important.

Like the Yang-tse-kiang, in China, the Mississippi River will have on its banks great centres of interior trade; and the Mississippi States, which are like unto nations in size and resources, will add millions on millions to prosperous population, where no foreign enemy can invade, where no domestic traitor can distract, and where political union is political life everlasting. There will be more millions of inhabitants in the Mississippi basin than any nation of the earth now contains, not between the Indus River and the Yellow Sea.

Among genuine political economists, the housewife, who, with a few dollars a week, received out of her husband's earnings, keeps her household together, everything neat and tidy in appearance, and sends her children to school week-day and Sunday, is supreme over speculators in theories, inflationists who collapse credit, and jugglers who abuse charters.

If Stephen Girard and the founder of the Astors could take a "bird's-eye" view of New York and Philadelphia, what estimate would they put on the *bonus* element in railway finance?

The oak develops from an acorn through a century of time, whereas, after a shower, a mushroom matures in a night: the charter-clad juggler can chloroform his conscience and magnetize his finger nerves; but, though guano will quicken the ground, it will not serve for sunshine to ripen grain fit for harvest; and however fiction may entertain its readers, it is base and dishonest to substitute it for truth in book accounts, official reports, or anywhere else.

A province in America is not a political body in embryo, with a head crowned in prospective. The royal toy brought disaster to its two temporary wearers south of Texas; and in the history which repeated itself in Mexico is a lesson not to be left out of the calculations of any royal sprig or sprout ambitious to wear a crown and found a dynasty in North America; for the new world is insulated from the old by three thousand miles of Atlantic Ocean, which is a ferry for immigration and intertrade, and likewise a barrier to marplots with political plans and enemies with deadly weapons. The immigrant and tourist are welcomed over its waves, and for the premeditated destroyer of liberty there are greedy monsters in its depths.

As the branches of a tree converge in its trunk, so the branches of the Caucasian race, from the continent and islands **of Europe, come** together **in wedlock in the** American Union, **where those who followed** since Columbus discovered have peopled a new **country and established** a new power between two seas, with a dozen doors open to Europe for immigration and exportation, and a "golden gate" open to Asia for intertrade in commodities of commerce. And if Great Britain, as a nation in Europe, would be *entente cordiale* with the United States, it only need first and primarily to leave the Dominion of Canada to the option of **its in**dwellers, each province to determine its own **future transition to a** State of the Union.

Whilst Great Britain is on this side of the Atlantic, in provinces **across the** American main **and** islands on its coasts, the United States must **construe its** asseverations of distinguished consideration, and all **that,** with a mental reservation, and not cease to remember that the English dictionary is prolific of words which supply diplomacy with a vocabulary, and which, in **the** statutes, are made to mean what **the** judge on the bench says they express, in his opinion.

Towards the United States, Russia, on the other hand, has never shown equivocal friendship, **nor** been guilty of collusion with an enemy in time of war, civil or foreign. And, as a logical sequence, behold with **what** reciprocity and cordiality the United States and Russia clasp and shake hands across Behring Strait, **from** the shores **of** Kamtschatka and Alaska!

In the suppression of the mutiny and attempted revolution in **India** in 1857, a movement inspired by love of country, Great **Britain** transported the King **of Delhi** to where he soon died, **and killed his** son and grandson, and so extinguished the royal line of legitimate successors of the great Moguls; for the King of Delhi was the head of the Mogul empire and a potentate of ancient lineage and illustrious rank among Hindoos and Mussulmans. But in **British** eyes it was a crime to be a native legitimist **in** Hindostan; and because the King of Delhi was the descendant of the Mogul emperors who had ruled over a vast empire before India was distracted into petty sovereignties, therefore the King of Delhi was considered dangerous to British supremacy in India, and so the King of Delhi was doomed to transportation and inevitable death, and his son and grandson were deprived of life in opposition to a divine commandment and in mockery of manhood justice; and this satanic cruelty was practiced so that there should be no legal representative alive in **Hindostan** to reign over the Mogul empire revived, in case the natives of India should unite in an effort to expel their foreign oppressors and reëstablish home rule. In other words, the **royal line** of Delhi was **exterminated to prevent** the restoration of a time-honored Mogul regime in India, adverse to British rule. And Rajahs, Khans, and other native dignitaries were hanged in 1857, **for** political reasons, by the British in India, where the "king of beasts" is considerate and merciful to other animals of inferior capabilities for defence, contrasted with the satraps of the nation that carries the lion on its coat of arms, and makes "British interests" a justification of conquest for trade and a plea for acquisition of territory for colonial empire around the globe; especially in places where subjugation is practicable through diplomacy and subsidy, where spoliation is profitable, and uncivilized population is defenceless against treaty translations and modern guns.

In antiquity of civilization Hindostan long antedates Great Britain; and the old plea of the Christianity of Great Britain is no longer available, since its intrigue against the San Stefano treaty to prolong the stay of the Turk in Europe, and its acceptance of Cyprus Island as subsidy for a defensive alliance with the Mahometan power that centuries ago crossed over from Asia to Europe and waged war against the Christian nations to exterminate the Christian religion. Except for the interference of Great Britain, the Turk would have been scourged out of Europe, for Austria, without British coöperation, was impotent to act against Russia. And so Austria and Great Britain, both jealous of Russia, and both greedy for spoils, conspired against the Christians in European Turkey, for their own mutual aggrandizement. And now, with the San Stefano treaty between Russia and Turkey, the Berlin Congress of the seven powers, and the defensive alliance between Great Britain and Turkey, known to mankind of all religions, the hypocrisy and selfishness of Great Britain are of record in evidence that will endure in history to confront professions contrary to acts. Review Lord Beaconsfield, the British hero in these diplomatic exploits, and wherein is there proof of sincerity, truthfulness, or statesmanship, that will stand the test of honest criticism, in his sharp practice, which must not be confounded with policy farsighted?

Considered as a finality for Europe, in the interests of peace, the Berlin Congress was a failure, because it settled only a few of the minor and adjourned most of the main issues of the questions it was called together to discuss, arbitrate and solve, for a time to be measured not by days but by years. But before the ambassadors had been absent a month from Berlin, behold Austria meeting with resistance, and made to pay with the blood of its soldiery for its trespass in Bosnia and Herzegovina.

The **Berlin** Congress partitioned two provinces of Turkey to Austria, a non-combatant in the war between Russia and Turkey; but when Austria marched into the territory allotted to it as its prize for co-operation with Great Britain, **first** against Russia in the Bulgaria of the San Stefano treaty, and last against Turkey in Bosnia and Herzegovina, then the people portioned off made defensive war against **invasion,** and Austrian prestige lost the shine put on it at Berlin with a British brush. Austria can only rule **where she can conquer.** For preserving it from dismemberment in 1849, Austria **in 1878** repaid Russia with ingratitude. But Servia is an independent nation, and Hungary may yet regain its independence of Austria. There remains much for diplomacy and the sword to do in the basin of the **Danube River and south of** the Balkan Mountains.

Since Russia obtained a frontier on the Black Sea at the Knieper in 1774, that power, previously bounded by the Caspian and **the** Baltic, has made one acquisition after another along the Black Sea shores in Europe and Asia, till now its entire northern and eastern coasts and parts of its western and southern coasts belong to Russia, which has regained Bessarabia and added Batoum to its harbors and Kars to its strongholds. Nor can nor will Russia cease to acquire territory or influence on the Black Sea, till it shall have acquired ground essential for the protection of its commerce in the free navigation of the Bosphorus and the Dardanelles to the Ægean Sea via Constantinople, as **the** United States enjoy between the Mississippi River **system** and the Gulf of Mexico via New Orleans. True, wars have procrastinated Russia's progress, but meanwhile Russia has expanded and developed into a colossal power that will not be content nor satisfied until the straits between Europe and Asia, which the Turks have too long straddled, are open to its ships, and it can protect its commerce to the Mediterranean Sea.

It would not be tolerated in Denmark to blockade or embargo the **sound or belt to the Baltic; nor** in Great Britain to blockade or embargo the Strait of Gibraltar nor the English Channel. And a frontage **on** the straits between the Black Sea and the Mediterranean is as essential to Russia as Florida to the United States, Dover to England, Calais to France.

England covets Egypt and the Euphrates valley, because they contain routes to India from the Mediterranean, and acquired Cyprus Island **because of its** strategic significance as a naval station, with

reference to the Suez Canal and Euphrates railway routes to India; and at the same time and **with** the same breath cants about Russian aggression, and strives to **keep** that power out of Constantinople. The words "British interests" would serve the devil for a short motto in pandemonium, as it does for politicians in London, who barter away the Christian Church **in** Turkey to save the British dollar **in** India and elsewhere. Great is the dollar in Britain.

For whatever the United States may deem necessary of enactment **and execution to** prevent the establishment of dynastic government in Canada, it has the supreme and all-sufficient law of self-preservation, additional to precedents in the practice of Great Britain **where it** considered its interests prospectively involved. And if British fleets in past times had terrors to nations with small navies and imperfect defences, in present time the British iron-clad is impotent to bulldoze the torpedo, which is as destructive to an iron-clad ship of war as to a wooden target. In the account between the Russian torpedo and the Turkish iron-clad the credit balance is largely in favor of the torpedo. The role of the iron-clad is rather to menace with demonstrations than attack with projectiles; for the torpedo charged to explode **is more to** be **dreaded than a floating** battery in an iron-clad ship, **which is vulnerable in the same** proportion that it was claimed to be invulnerable. **A weather vane is** put up to point to the wind and turn when the wind **changes; and** public opinion weighs with weights in a true balance and turns on a pivot in gravity's centre. Hence, on examination it **is easy to** ascertain which way the wind blows, and **in** what direction public opinion tends. Concealment of the truth is impossible where discussion winnows assertions from facts. That the iron-clad has disappointed expectation in Europe is a truth patent to everybody and a special **grief to** Englishmen, because there can be no naval supremacy whilst the torpedo, if not paramount in the waters, **is** a terror **to iron-clads.** And to show how the British navy chicaned at Copenhagen in 1801, at Algiers in 1816, and at Acre in 1840, the following extract is copied from page 271 of Col. J. P. Chesney's "Russo-Turkish campaigns of 1828 and 1829," published in 1854, in the beginning of the war against Russia by France, Great Britain, and Sardinia, as allies of Turkey, four powers against one; a war in which the British, after more than one trial, did not take the Redan, though the French did take the Malakhoff; whereupon the Russians retired **to** the north forts of Sebastopol and were not driven thence **by the besieging allies.**

Col. Chesney, R. **A.,** D. C. **L.,** F. R. S., says:

"It is true that three remarkable instances have occurred in modern times, which may seem to favor the superiority of ships over stone walls. These are Copenhagen, Algiers and Acre. In the **first case,** it is understood that Nelson was only relieved from a critical situation by sending a letter on shore, which caused the batteries of Copenhagen to cease firing against the fleet.

"In the second instance, **the** attack on **Algiers** was made during a state of peace. We know that after our fleet **had** entered the harbor, **not in** line of battle, but almost ship by ship, and, consequently, greatly exposed to the garrison, the *Queen Charlotte*, by the advice of an engineer officer, Sir William Ried, K. C. B., now the distinguished Governor of Malta, was placed with her broadside on the flank of **the grand or mole** battery. The rest of the fleet had also taken up advantageous positions without a shot being fired by the garrison, until Lord Exmouth waved his hat as the signal for the fleet to open its fire simultaneously.

"In the third case, that of Acre, the fleet was also allowed to take up positions which had been previously arranged, without any opposition. Buoys had even been placed beforehand, and what **had been** a state of peace up to that moment was only broken by the **opening** of a terrific fire of shells and shot, when everything was ready;—**at least on our** side."

British duplicity, however, practiced in its naval tactics at Copenhagen, Algiers and Acre, as described by a **competent British military** authority, a colonel in the Royal Artillery, did **not avail at Sebastopol,** the siege of which was commenced by **a joint** attack of the allied fleets and forces, October 17, 1854, which was unsuccessful; nor was **the** Malakhoff taken by the French till September 8, 1855, **when the allies entered that** portion of Sebastopol left **in ruins by** the retiring Russians. Neither did the Baltic fleet, under Sir C. Napier, venture to attack Cronstadt, which defends St. Petersburg, in the Russo-Turkish-French-British-Sardinian war of 1853–1856, a war which was waged to wrest from Russia the Crimea and other **ground, but** which ended leaving Russia intact, save that its Bessarabian **corner was cut off, till it** was retroceded **by** the San Stefano treaty, a retrocession which the Congress of **Berlin** confirmed. The Crimean war added no prestige to Russia's allied enemies. To Great Britain it was a loss of prestige. The war **of** 1877–1878, ended **by the treaty of** San Stefano, between Russia and Turkey, conferred a lustre on Russia's arms which the Congress of Berlin did not dim nor eclipse with its own performances.

CHAPTER IX.

On the 29th July, 1878, it was officially announced, in London, that the Marquis of Lorne, son-in-law of Queen Victoria, had been appointed Governor-General of the Dominion of Canada, successor to Lord Dufferin. The Marquis of Lorne, husband of the Princess Louise, is the eldest son of the Duke of Argyll. He was born August 6, 1845, and was married March 21, 1871. The Princess Louise, the sixth of the nine children of Queen Victoria and Prince Albert, was born March 18, 1848. The Marquis of Lorne, whose mission it is to vivisect the Dominion of Canada with royal blood, and attempt the task of founding a dynasty in the shadow of the tree of liberty, in soil near its roots, which are sound like its branches, is a member of Parliament from the county of Argyll, Scotland. The county of Argyll is positively liberal in its politics, and the Marquis of Lorne, who comes to America probably to propagate royalty in disguise, perchance in expectation of a propitious season to declare a kingdom, professed liberal sentiments when he was elected to Parliament; but after his marriage to a daughter of the Queen, whereby the subject was flattered with a condescension singular in the sovereign, he acted with the Tories as unconditionally as if he had never given a pledge to his Liberal constituency in Argyll. The Marquis, therefore, is a British diplomatist, who, when he says one thing, perhaps means another. But, in America, the art of government is open to universal study; and the intelligent elector who knows how to wield the ballot and to strike with it, contemplates a royalist with as little awe as a learned physician looks on the medicine man of an Indian tribe. In republican eyes king-craft is a transparent sham, and a royal court is but a theatre with a stage and a stock company. For star actors in political parts do we not search among distinguished ministers who served crowned heads? Is not Shakspeare immortal in the realm of mind beyond the royal characters depicted in his plays? Does not revolution uproot a dynasty as a tornado uproots a tree? And where the tree stood before the storm destroyed it, does not the ploughman make a furrow and plant seed to utilize the ground, and so turn a visitation in wind to advantage in agriculture? Is not a fire in a city a blessing in flame when a site is cleared for needed improvements not otherwise attainable, because of opposition against tearing down old structures, superseded and depreciated? Forces in nature are not diminished because now and then a storm makes a commotion in the air, and there is destruction on land and sea. After a thunder-storm the atmosphere is more exhilarating; and after a plot against nationality and free government is exploded, the political sky of a progressive people resumes its normal azure hue. The sky of Mexico was twice overcast with cloud, but it is a third time cerulean, if not serene.

The Republic in France was twice supplanted, but now France is a Republic for the third time, watchful and determined not to be again betrayed in the interest of legitimacy, dynasty or empire, three forms of personal government antagonistic to republicanism, because birthright succession to a sceptre is contrary to the right of the governed to choose the chief of the government.

The masses, in America, understand their interests, political, educational, religious and pecuniary, too well, and comprehend the situation and its surroundings too clearly, to tolerate a kingdom or an empire in North America, or permit a plotting power in Europe to intrigue against the annexation of free States to the American Union; a century plant, which, on its hundredth anniversary, in 1876, blossomed in Fairmount Park, Philadelphia, with thirty-eight States, and bore eleven territorial buds on its branches. Royalty is a vine which exhales a poison, deadly where it causes sleep, shelters parasites where it creeps and covers, and kills the tree it girdles and overgrows, as the stumps of punk fungus, only fit for tinder, in the genealogical park testify. In truth, it was an error to import the English sparrow into the United States, where it is out of place among singing birds, that make the country and the town vocal with native songs. The British tramp, with wings, has a voracity in disproportion to its size. And among more musical American birds in prettier plumage, the sparrow is the equivalent of the communist in the French republic, and is an importation to the United States "not fit to be made."

American citizens who study the political weather and consult probabilities in British politics, will not fraternize with title bearers imported into Canada to act automatic parts in a game of dynastic chess played in London against free institutions in America. Let exhibitions of loyalty to royalty come from the St. George societies, whose members are imbued with British ideas in fast colors, visible through the ink of a naturalization certificate!

The worthy Princess Louise, now the Marchioness of Lorne, is not more worthy than Nellie Grant, now Mrs. Sartoris. And did not Harriet Lane, now Mrs. Johnson, do the honors of the White House, in Washington, with as much grace and dignity as any princess in her appropriate part in Windsor Castle? The law of quality which pervades American oysters and eggs, and causes their classification into "good" and "bad," also pervades the titled and untitled ranks in Europe, where those who pass for "commons" show as large a percentage of "good" as the so-called nobility.

Is a princess lovelier than another lady in a bathing-suit, in the breakers at Cape May and Rockaway? And as from the time of Eve's first pregnancy nature has used but one common mould for the reproduction of the human species, it follows that the process of maternity is the same everywhere, and that the assumptions of superiority in birth—and a birth is the delivery of a life to the world by a matrix of single standard established by nature in universal law— are unfounded in physiology and false in everything; also, that distinctions and discriminations made to the advantage of titled and the disadvantage of untitled persons are abuses in human government which will not be permitted in North America, where there is no road open for royalty to travel in safety to a throne; and where, moreover, two royal roads commenced in Mexico both led to places of execution.

"The Bourbons learn nothing and forget nothing." Are all dynastic families like the Bourbons? And is not a minister of state who cannot discern that dynastic government is destined to perish like other impostures of the past based on superstition, which is everywhere disappearing from political horizons, unfit for office in these latter advanced days? Animal nature, nowhere perfect, may be found as near perfection where all are citizens as where titles and honors are hereditary and succession is independent of merit. No, no; human nature is not compounded like bronze preparatory to casting a statue in a mould, nor like metal in a bell, impregnated with silver to soften its sound. Greater monsters or worse men never lived on the earth than some of the occupants of the throne of England. And criminal calendars show that a prince can be as wicked as a peasant. Away then with the arrogance that hereditary office exalts human nature, which, where it attains to highest exaltation in public and private life, is always founded on manhood and womanhood, worth and virtue. The citizen reserves his veneration and his adoration for the one universal God, and makes allotment of his respect and admiration according to his understanding, experience and observation, with mental impartiality and without preference, prejudice, or bias.

The British political system, which perpetuates power in a privileged class, and tolerates the laws of primogeniture and entail, positive drawbacks to reform, has made London a mammoth and mastodon city, has made the dozen millionaires and the million companions of poverty "acquainted with grief."

The spectacle of honor in plumes and ribbons and decorations on breasts and shoulders ennobled by partial law, not by impartial justice and honest effort, does not fill the requirements of manhood nor satisfy the educated mind, quick to discern and able to weigh, measure and appreciate. The smell of food flavored for the palace does not appease the hunger of the multitude in hovels, for the stomach is sensitive and the body must have nourishment. To provide things to eat and to wear is a common duty, for food and clothing are common necessaries; and hence opportunities for sustentation and betterment ought to be open to everybody.

Wide, indeed, is the difference between a citizen and a subject, a republic in the hands of republican citizens and a monarchy administered by a dynasty, with an army to enforce its decrees; particularly to the masses who work with brain and muscle, operate with mind on matter, and among whom are a considerable proportion who have ideas to embody in practical use and aspirations to realize, through rewards in sight of manly ambition and within reach of honest effort.

The annual grants received by the Queen of Great Britain and Ireland and the members of her family amount to a very large sum, about three million dollars, for the royal household of Great Britain is a numerous family, which derives its main consideration not from services rendered to the kingdom since the House of Hanover obtained the succession through George I., but from the circumstance that it supplies the sovereign on the throne and reigns by authority of law, without contest—a great matter—and with the sanction of Parliament, the Lords and Commons.

The House of Hanover began its reign with George I., 1714, when the American colonies were in the infancy of development; but neither of the four Georges, who reigned jointly one hundred and six years, nor William IV., who died June 20, 1837, was more than an ordinary mortal, considered apart from the crown, which invests its wearer with official patronage and royal prerogatives and rights.

Queen Victoria, distinguished for her domestic virtues and motherly merits, and for the higher standard established in her court, and who personally commands the respect and the affectionate good-will of the *people* of the United States, was crowned at Westminster June 28, 1838. Queen Victoria, only daughter of the Duke of Kent, was born May 24, 1819; was married to her cousin, Prince Albert of Saxe-Coburg, February 10, 1840; Prince Albert died December 14, 1861, lamented and mourned. As the issue of woman born into the world with life is nowhere exempted from death, the common penalty imposed by nature, there is a democratic condition in the child born naked into the world, in helplessness and dependence, and a democratic condition in the hereditary potentate when death levels him down on his back to die like his subject, and mingle his dust with universal humanity in common mother earth. All men, therefore, are born democrats and die democrats, wherefore democracy, primitive and pure in nature, where party name cannot corrupt, is the normal condition of the beginning and ending of man's sojourn in the society to which he owes service, in the years of his responsibility between youth and age, when the vigor of manhood, which includes all of life but its ends, fits him for duty. The superiority claimed for royalty is a mockery of spirituality with materialism. Did not the Son of God say, "My kingdom is not of this world"? It was the mission of Jesus Christ to redeem the world from the penalty of its sin and assure to mankind a possible higher life in a spiritual sphere, where material matters cannot be perverted to confound the masses by arch diplomatists, lawyers, and mercenaries; such as abound in the old world at this present juncture of abrasion among the branches of the race founded by Adam, saved from drowning by Noah, and made progressive by the inspired words of the Saviour, who was crucified because he preached against temporal kingdom. Love of splendor was the ruin of the Jews, who loved glitter better than God. And wherein is London better than Jerusalem, for does not London covet empire and lust for conquest?

In proportion as intelligence is spread among the people, crowns will be shorn of their prerogatives, which in most cases are usurpations, and written constitutions will restrict incumbents of office within limits. Contrast the caskets which contain the dust of departed kings who reigned by dynastic birthright, with the slab that covers the grave of a patriot, author, discoverer, or inventor, conspicuous in human annals.

Go into Westminster Abbey, and observe how visitors search in the Poet's Corner for names perennial in the reader's mind and immortal in the world of letters. Is not England more indebted to ministers of state than to its kings and queens? Is it not notorious that her Majesty's ministers managed the Crown, manipulated the Porte, and ignored the Houses of Parliament (albeit the Commons ought and might exercise a controlling influence in the realm), in the negotiation and ratification of the Treaty of Defensive Alliance with Turkey, signed June 4, 1878, and amended July 1, twenty-six days thereafter? Why, then, as the Crown of England is cast in a subordinate part in the practice of England, where the ministry usurps the functions of government in making treaties with foreign powers, wherein prospective war is made probable, are the princes and princesses of the House of Hanover, a German graft, exalted in official and social honors over the sons and daughters of Englishmen, distinguished for service to their country?

Contemplate the Commonwealth under Cromwell, as a power among nations, with the monarchy under Charles II. and his successors! Princes and princesses are men and women born in lawful wedlock, like citizens and subjects, *nothing more.* Nor does their so-called royal birth entitle them to consideration, social or political, over the sons and daughters of the President or Presidentess in Washington.

In the United States the President relapses into the citizen, and his children blend in the society of the common country, as raindrops disappear in a river. And so with prince and princess, husband and wife, who come over from Europe to hold office in Canada. The Governor-General and his wife are official characters, entitled to the consideration awarded to unexceptionable persons in distinguishing office. And if the Duke of Argyll so administers his office as to win admiration of his modesty and respect for his talents, he will earn a name that will emit a lustre which cannot be borrowed from a title.

The American Union has developed very many distinguished men, who exalted the official rank in which they served their country, and whose names fill the offices they held with honorable associations. But because an American citizen is made a president, a general, senator, or ambassador, to perform a duty for a compensation, with opportunity to stimulate the official to win fame and deserve gratitude, success under such circumstances is not a reason for a grant or inheritance to his children; for the citizen is under obligation to discharge his duty, and for simply doing his duty no one is entitled to extra praise; although for service measured by merit, the American people are prone and prompt to award praise, in ways more substantial than words.

The moon has no atmosphere, and consequently shines without a mist. The American citizen has no title, and is judged on his character and record. A title is a veil and so is a cloud; but a veil like a cloud is only a temporary obscuration, for a cloud will pass away on the wind and a veil is a penetrable disguise to penetrating eyes. Hence the title-wearer, like the weather overhead, must withstand observation and criticism. Like the stars in space, officials in titles must undergo scrutiny through the telescope, for the constituent is an astronomer given to exact calculation.

An envelope is not a letter. In a republic a title is no more than a counterfeit bank note. And if Great Britain would capitalize its aristocracy at the par of its self-estimated value and then appraise it at what it is worth to the realm, in the opinion of experts appointed to detect and expose fraud, it would be shown that the Turkish loan is not the largest nominal asset of Great Britain.

The Marquis of Lorne, the husband of the Princess Louise and son-in-law of the Queen of Great Britain and Ireland, and Empress of India, as supplemented by Lord Beaconsfield, is Governor-General of the Dominion of Canada, in the service of a foreign country with which the nation of the United States has great and grave reasons for dissatisfaction and displeasure; nor will these reasons cease to acquire force from current facts, till the British government discontinues its plots in America, where its designs are as intelligible as if printed in its London programme.

INDEX.

	PAGE
Acre, British Fleet at,	80
Alaska,	30, 33, 39, 62, 76
Algiers, British Fleet at,	80
America, no Dynasty in,	21, 64, 75
Ammon, R. A., Brakeman at Pittsburgh,	52
Area of the American Union,	20
Austria,	9, 11, 44, 46, 51, 67, 77
Baltimore and Ohio Railroad,	6
Berlin, Congress of,	9, 40, 47, 50, 67, 77
Black Sea once a Turkish Lake,	11, 46, 78
Boundary Line,	10, 33, 37
British Columbia,	5, 14, 21, 27
British Navy at Copenhagen, Algiers and Acre,	79
Buffalo, City of,	12, 23
Canada, Dominion of,	3, 6, 13, 23, 27, 33, 66
Canada, Governor-General of,	81
Canada Grand Trunk Railway,	38
Canada Pacific Railway,	5, 24, 27, 37
Cartier, Jacques,	5
Chicago,	24, 38, 75
Citizens and Subjects,	7, 15, 28, 62, 66, 70, 82
Delhi Dynasty exterminated,	76
Divine Right of Kings, Fiction of,	62
Dynasty, not in North America,	7, 21, 25, 28, 46, 63, 66, 75
England,	48, 67, 69, 78
English Tactics in America,	60
Erie Canal,	16, 23
Fiction of Divine Right of Kings,	62
Florida,	33
Foreign Trade of the United States,	71, 72
Fort Bourbon, afterwards York Fort,	6
France,	8, 12, 32, 37, 42, 46, 50, 53
Germany,	11, 51, 63, 65
Grant, General U. S.,	39, 52
Great Britain,	16, 35, 39, 41, 48, 58
Gulf of Mexico,	43
Halifax Fishery Award,	40
House of Hanover,	84
Hudson Bay,	5, 12, 35, 39
Hudson Bay Company,	12, 37
Indelible Names,	53, 67
India, Suppression of Mutiny in,	41, 76
Ireland, population of,	58
Italy,	11, 44, 50

	PAGE
Lake Erie,	16, 22
Lake Superior,	6, 23, 34
Lake Traverse,	17, 22
Lake Winnipeg,	4, 17, 22, 32, 39
London,	13, 59, 74
Louisiana,	11, 26, 32, 62
Maine,	15
Malakhoff and Redan at Sebastopol,	80
Manitoba,	6, 26, 33, 68
Mexico,	4, 21, 64, 75
Middle Sea,	27, 36, 39
Minnesota,	6, 20, 22
Minnesota River Valley,	17, 22
Mississippi, Basin of the,	19, 69
Mutiny in India,	76
Nelson River,	26
New Boundary between Manitoba and Ontario,	33
New Brunswick and Maine,	15
New York City,	59, 69
Nova Scotia and Massachusetts,	15
Ontario, Province of,	33
Original Thirteen States,	36, 62
Pennsylvania Railroad,	6
Philadelphia,	69
Philadelphia Soldiers at Pittsburgh,	55
Pittsburgh,	55
Population,	6, 58, 64
Population, Nativities of,	65
Public Opinion the paramount power,	25
Railroad Distances,	24
Railway Expansion in six years,	73
Red River of the North,	17, 23, 39
Republic of France,	8, 12, 45, 53, 63
Revulsion of 1873, some of the Causes of,	72
Riot **not** Insurrection,	56
Russia,	9, 42, 47, 50, 78
Saint Paul,	18, 23
San Juan Island **Arbitration**,	40
Serlick Settlement,	5, 37
Shoes not flanged in America,	7
Spain,	44, 51
St. Lawrence River,	14, 24, 43
St. Louis,	44
Texas,	26, 31
Thirteen Original States,	36, 62
Trade of the United States,	71, 72
Transvaal Republic,	62
Traverse Lake Summit,	17
Turkey,	9, 45, 50, 67, 78
United States,	3, 10, 13, 19, 39, 51, 65, 86
Vienna, Congress of,	10, 40
Washington Territory,	5, 21
Washington Treaty of 1871,	39, 59
West, the, bound by Hudson Bay and Gulf of Mexico,	18, 35
Western States, when admitted into the Union,	19
Western Territories, when organized,	20

www.ingramcontent.com/pod-product-compliance
Lightning Source LLC
Chambersburg PA
CBHW020300090426
42735CB00009B/1152